SHAPED BY GOD'S HEART

OTHER LEADERSHIP NETWORK TITLES

The Ascent of a Leader: How Ordinary Relationships Develop Extraordinary Character and Influence, by Bill Thrall, Bruce McNicol, and Ken McElrath

The Elephant in the Boardroom: Speaking the Unspoken about Pastoral Transitions by Carolyn Weese and J. Russell Crabtree

The Leader's Journey: Accepting the Call to Personal and Congregational Transformation, by Jim Herrington, Robert Creech, and Trisha Taylor

Leading Congregational Change: A Practical Guide for the Transformational Journey, by Jim Herrington, Mike Bonem, and James H. Furr

Leading Congregational Change Workbook, by James H. Furr, Mike Bonem, and Jim Herrington

Leading the Team-Based Church: How Pastors and Church Staffs Can Grow Together into a Powerful Fellowship of Leaders, by George Cladis

The Millennium Matrix: Reclaiming the Past, Reframing the Future of the Church, by M. Rex Miller

A New Kind of Christian: A Tale of Two Friends on a Spiritual Journey, by Brian McLaren

The Present Future: Six Tough Questions for the Church, by Reggie McNeal

The Story We Find Ourselves in: Further Adventures of a New Kind of Christian, by Brian McLaren

A Work of Heart, by Reggie McNeal

SHAPED BY GOD'S HEART

*The Passion and Practices
of Missional Churches*

Milfred Minatrea

JOSSEY-BASS
A Wiley Imprint
www.josseybass.com

Published by Jossey-Bass
A Wiley Imprint
989 Market Street, San Francisco, CA 94103-1741   www.josseybass.com

Jossey-Bass books and products are available through most bookstores. To contact
Jossey-Bass directly call our Customer Care Department within the U.S. at 800-956-7739,
outside the U.S. at 317-572-3986 or fax 317-572-4002.

Jossey-Bass also publishes its books in a variety of electronic formats. Some content that
appears in print may not be available in electronic books.

Unless otherwise noted, Scripture quotations taken from the New American Standard
Bible®, Copyright © 1960, 1962, 1963, 1968, 1971, 1972, 1973, 1975, 1977, 1995 by
The Lockman Foundation Used by permission. (www.Lockman.org)

Library of Congress Cataloging-in-Publication Data

  Minatrea, Milfred.
    Shaped by God's heart: the passion and practices of missional churches /
Milfred Minatrea.
      p. cm.
    Includes bibliographical references.
    ISBN 0-7879-7111-1 (alk. paper)
    1. Mission of the church. I. Title.
  BV601.8.M57 2004
  253—dc22   2004006648

Printed in the United States of America
FIRST EDITION
HB Printing   10 9 8 7 6 5 4 3 2 1

CONTENTS

111325

PART THREE
Structures and Strategies for Becoming Missional   **141**

PREFACE:
A PERSONAL LETTER TO THE READER

AFTER MORE THAN TWENTY YEARS of serving Christ, I know that the church can also be a dynamic experience of personal transformation, where individuals connect with God in profoundly intimate and personal ways, and in a powerful corporate connection as a whole body. Together, members exhibit the power of God at work in their lives, making the church winsome to outsiders and influential in communities. This church is optimistic: it believes itself to be the dwelling of God, uniquely empowered by His Spirit, living the transformational reality of His Kingdom in contemporary society.

Yet for many His church has become not a place of relationship but merely a place where people gather for religious ceremonies. Members belong to the church just as they may belong to the Lions or Rotary Club. They go to church, but often they do not see themselves *as* the church. Even parishioners speak of the facilities where they meet as "the church." What was intended by God as a living Body has been reduced to bricks and mortar, a building made with hands.

What has happened?

Many churches are vestiges of a former community that long ago underwent significant change. Parishioners became part of a church when they first moved into a growing community. In church, they established enduring relationships with people who held similar values. Their children were confirmed, baptized, and married in those sacred places. As the community changed across the years, members sold their homes and moved away. Yet they continued to drive back each week to enjoy the web of relationships that was their church, their dearest friends. They continued to worship but lost touch with the community around them. Increasingly, church became isolated from the world rather than engaged with the world.

As mission—the purpose of inviting and equipping individuals to be authentic disciples of Christ—gave way to maintenance of the status quo, people have grown weary of going through the motions of religious trappings without experiencing personal intimacy with God. Our world is filled with individuals whose lives manifest their deep hunger for something more than the nominal religious experiences they have observed thus far. They know something more exists; they just do not know how to get there. They search for a different type of church—and that church *does* exist today.

This church is not limited by geography or denomination. It is found across the globe in an increasing number of places where leaders have been willing to lose everything to gain something that was almost lost. They have caught a glimpse of God and are unwilling to settle for anything less than intimate relationship with Him. In this pursuit, they are rediscovering the authentic relationship that develops among fellow pilgrims on that path, members together in the Body of Christ. Those churches are preparing members, and holding each other accountable, to live as representatives for God in their individual spheres of influence, in their world. These are missional churches, reproducing communities of authentic disciples, being equipped as missionaries sent by God, to live and proclaim His Kingdom in their world.

One might say this is a new kind of church, but I would say that it is some two thousand years old. It is reclaiming the intent for which Christ established His church. In many ways, contemporary society is very close to the first-century experience. It is pluralistic, profoundly spiritual, but not necessarily Christian. Major ethical issues challenge social structures. Global distribution of wealth favors a privileged few whose responsibility to exercise compassionate concern for those in poverty is often lost to a "me-first" mentality.

Yet the missional church is not a first-century church; it is a twenty-first-century church committed to use every means available to accomplish God's missional purpose in the earth. Such churches are connecting members intimately with God and involving them in His mission around the world. They use global communication and transportation systems to gain information and extend influence. They are not content simply to provide financial resources so that a few select individuals can be involved in global missions. They are on mission as individuals and as communities of faith.

The measure of a missional church is the transformational impact of its members' lives in their world. Their influence results in new followers of Christ, new communities of faith developing. They are reproducing communities—followers resulting in others following Christ, leaders producing new leaders, cells expanding to new cells, and churches starting new churches. It is impossible to separate the individual focus from the corporate endeavor. The church *is* what its members *are*.

Shaped by God's Heart is the result of my observation of churches well on their way to being missional congregations. They are still forming and growing and changing. Each church is unique, yet all share common practices and ways of approaching the world. In this book, I have attempted to portray what a missional church looks like. My intent is not to create a model or models that you or other church leaders should seek to emulate. Rather, I hope that having seen what missional churches look like in other places, you may be led to observe your own church in this light. I hope that you, as a leader, will not leave your congregation, but rather influence it to become a life-giving missional community of authentic disciples.

I long for you to experience the depth of joy known only to those who abandon everything in pursuit of God and His purpose. My purpose in writing *Shaped by God's Heart* is to touch a place deep within you, a place marked by a profound desire to experience God in a most personal way intended for His Body, the Church.

To Pam,
Best friend in the journey toward His heart

ACKNOWLEDGMENTS

EACH OF US IS THE PRODUCT of many individuals who have shaped our lives. A book is no different. *Shaped by God's Heart* is a compendium of the influence and investment of countless thousands of persons who have marked my spiritual journey. I thank God for the foundation laid by a father who lived Christianity in his business and a mother who epitomizes generosity. My sister Ann, whose mobility and capacity to communicate have been severely limited by cerebral palsy, taught me to see the beauty of the individual within. One day soon she will run, dance, and sing for the first time in her life, a heavenly moment she awaits with eager anticipation.

So many parts of the Body of Christ have shaped me, as well. I am thankful for these Texas congregations who have allowed me to journey with them toward the heart of God: First and Denman Avenue in Lufkin; Meadowbrook and First in Irving; Colonial, Park Central, and Grace Temple in Dallas; and First in Lancaster. These churches and their staff members have taught me so much about the Father's Kingdom.

Wonderful colleagues in ministry have walked beside me in the shaping process. Dr. Bill Tinsley, Dr. E. B. Brooks, and Dr. Gary Hearon provided encouragement and mentoring, often without their own awareness. Their hearts reflect the heart of the Father. Rick Davis, Don Sewell, Dexton Shores, Bobby Smith, Jim Young, and Abe Zabaneh expanded my grasp of the coalescing of mission and ministry. Patty Lane and Lindsay Cofield each made significant contributions when I grew weary in the writing process.

The wonderful staff of the Missional Church Center has carried a heavier load while I was involved in research and writing. Thank you Fred Ater, Ted Elmore, Cindy Zoller, Maritza Solano, and Marla Bearden for offering your gifts so graciously in this process.

The Baptist General Convention of Texas and Dr. Charles Wade approved study leave that allowed me to focus on research. I am grateful for an environment in which research and writing are deemed essential. Thank you for your commitment to being Kingdom Christians.

Many friends made special contributions as *Shaped By God's Heart* came together. Frank Goodman gave me a key to his family's lake house with this invitation: "Use it as if it were your own." That setting was a beautiful retreat where many concepts first surfaced. In fact, I still have the key. Ernie Murray and Gaye Eichler cared enough to wade through and critique early drafts of the manuscript. I am grateful for their gracious assistance.

Carol Childress, formerly of Leadership Network, is a person I have long admired. Her encouragement that I pursue writing a portrait of missional churches fanned an original spark. The relationship between Leadership Network and Jossey-Bass introduced me to wonderfully capable new friends. I am thankful to Sheryl Fullerton, Catherine Craddock, Andrea Flint, and Sachie Jones for walking me through publishing processes that were foreign to me. Naomi Lucks Sigal was indispensable when I needed her gifts and expertise the most.

I am grateful to my family. My wife and best friend, Pam, never doubted this project was something God wanted me to accomplish. She prayed and encouraged. Likewise my children and their families in special ways gave me fuel for the journey. Thank you Kish, Corina, and Olivia; Allison, Andrew, and Ashtyn; and Joshua.

To every congregation and leader whose stories appear on these pages, thank you for treating me as an honored guest. Those who invited me into their churches and homes are now part of my family.

Finally, I am grateful to the Rev. David White of Victoria, Australia. On the day I began my research journey, we met on an Amtrak coach. We spent hours visiting about the Kingdom and ministry. Before we parted, he challenged me, "Do not just start this book. Finish it!" The page on which I wrote his comment in my journal is now dog-eared. David, thanks for that departing word. It served its purpose.

INTRODUCTION:
SENDING THE CHURCH INTO THE WORLD

JOHN SITS IN HIS STUDY, staring at the wall but looking nowhere. *Surely there is something more to ministry than this,* he says to himself. He recalls the excitement he felt when he first sensed God's call to ministry. Now he's worried about the couple who say they're thinking about taking their family to a church that can "better meet their needs." He'd like to talk to them more about it, but he's got Sunday School vacancies to fill, a Bible study to plan for, sermons to prepare, and calls to return. Is this really what he signed up for?

Most members, sensing his unease, reassure him that the church is going really well. They love their pastor and his faithfulness in caring for them, and it shows. Attendance grows steadily from year to year, and there's enough money to fund programs that they enjoy. The area around the facility shows the wear of a community past its prime, and the church properties, although well kept, are dated. Sure, upkeep is a constant challenge, but committees stay on top of it. They're also fairly satisfied with the overall program and ministry of the church: age-graded Bible study on Sunday mornings; youth activities, including the upcoming spring ski trip; good choral music, with vocalists who frequently use recorded tracks instead of piano or organ as accompaniment.

Still, deep inside, John feels his church slipping away from his grasp, and he knows that many of his colleagues are also struggling. Church attendance is largest on Sunday mornings, much smaller on Sunday evening, and pretty sparse on Wednesday nights.

When John asks members where the church could do better, some say that evangelism and outreach need attention. But only a few members are actively involved in outreach. Last fall, several members went through a witness-training course on Sunday evenings, but the church has no ongoing, organized, evangelistic emphasis. Mission organizations, once a strong part especially of children's ministry, are now hanging by a thread. Few attend the occasional mission meetings for men and women. At select times each year, members are encouraged to pray for and give to missions.

Goals are set for special offerings, and for a few weeks prayers include requests for those serving on "the mission fields." Members are faithful to give so that others may go.

In his study, reflecting on all this, John shakes his head. Maybe this is just how it is. He knows the church members are busy with their own lives and families. How can *he* do more? He barely has enough hours in the week to complete all the things on his to-do list as it is. He has good relationships with his members and the community. The church is stable. Why then does he feel that something is missing? That there should be something more?

John is not alone in his feelings. This question of what is missing plagues a lot of today's church leaders. The sheer quantity of activities involved in a church can wear everybody out. Such churches may be excellent social organizations, whose members enjoy relationship with one another, but they have little transformational impact within the local community.

When the activities of a church focus inward, the church has exchanged its mission for maintenance. There is a great difference between focus on mission and focus on maintenance, and there is a great difference in the impact each has in God's Kingdom. At its core, it is not the number of activities a church is involved in that defines success, but whether those activities result in accomplishing God's mission for His church. True success can only result when the activities of God's Body reflect what is in His heart.

A New Missional Church

As some of John's colleagues are discovering, there is in the world today a new kind of church forming. It is a church that reclaims its New Testament role with authenticity and energy and is not limited by denomination or location. In this book, I advocate for this *missional* church: a reproducing community of authentic disciples, being equipped as missionaries sent by God, to live and proclaim His Kingdom in their world.

In pursuing the missional vision, leaders seek to rediscover that for which the church was sent in the first century. In his magnificent work *Transforming Mission,* David Bosch explains this concept beautifully: "Mission was understood as being derived from the very nature of God. . . . Father, Son and Holy Spirit sending the church into the world . . . a movement from God to the world: . . . There is a church because there is a mission, not vice versa."[1]

Today, a handful of missional churches—here in the United States and elsewhere around the world—are breathing new life into the Body of Christ, finding renewed vitality as they abandon themselves to God's purpose in mission. In 2002, I was privileged to visit a number of these churches, experiencing their vitality for worship and enthusiasm for mission. They are not perfect—no church is. They are growing, experimenting with new forms, finding their way. They are living organisms, passionate in their commitment, and exceptional in their practice of focusing attention outward, beyond themselves.

The heart of this book looks at the distinctive passion and practices of missional churches. If you visit any missional church, you will see immediately that they do things differently from most other churches. As I observed missional churches for this book, I found—somewhat to my surprise—that nine distinct practices consistently surfaced. I also found that it was fairly easy for pastors and lay leaders to put these practices to work energizing their own congregations.

Shaped by God's Heart is intended for pastors like John as well as for lay leaders who seek positive change for their church communities. At the conclusion of each chapter, you will find exercises for reflection and application as well as resources for additional study in the same subject area. In Chapters Four through Twelve you will also find a Missional Practice Assessment tool you can use to assess how your church reflects the distinctive practice highlighted in the chapter. I hope you and your coleaders will also use the comprehensive Missional Practice Assessment tool in the Appendix to understand the willingness of your church to move to missional.

I hope too that this book will be a supplementary text for seminary courses in missions and church planting. Student formation must provide hope for a new kind of church—a church capable of making a significant difference in the lives of individuals and of society. Many students will serve existing churches, helping them to be shaped by God's heart. Others will plant new churches. The churches they begin will reflect the values they hold. Culture is behavior driven by underlying values. If students value missional culture, they will begin missional churches. I pray today's students will become architects of a pervasive missional church culture.

The Vast and Endless Sea

During the past year, I became enamored with this quote from Antoine de Saint-Exupéry: "If you want to build a ship, don't drum up the men to gather wood, divide the work, and give orders. Instead, teach them to yearn for the vast and endless sea."

I have spent more than twenty years helping churches develop methods to drum up men, gather wood, divide the work, and so on, and have had some success. But I have also learned that if churches are to accomplish God's purpose, they must do more than apply marketing principles: they must yearn for the vastness and endlessness of relationship with Him.

Most ecclesiological writings focus on structures and strategies, and these are important concerns. Still, the primary focus must be upon spirituality. Knowing His purpose informs strategies, which are the pathway to accomplishing purpose. Structures can then be developed that best facilitate the actions toward accomplishing determined strategies.

So the formula must be spirituality, then strategy, then structure. For many existing churches, long-established structures have become the forms through which any new endeavor must pass. If structures do not accommodate strategies, they destroy effectiveness. Mission is sacrificed at the altar of "the way we do things here." When existing structures do not enable new methods, those methods fail.

Missional churches arise from the foundations laid by the thousands of traditional churches that have supported and envisioned the modern missionary movement. As we move into a new age and the new paradigm that is now emerging, missional churches will flow naturally into areas conventional churches were not structured to address.

Before you begin *Shaped by God's Heart,* I want to say a word about what this book is *not.* It is not a book about personal transformation, and it is not intended as a theology of mission. It does encourage you first to ask a spiritual question: "What does God desire for our church? What is on His heart?" That should prompt a strategic question: "What would He have us to do, as individuals and as a Body?" Only then can you ask: "How should we structure our ministry to best accomplish those strategies?"

Shaped by God's Heart is a pragmatic observation of actual churches on mission, learning and growing, taking chances, being a new kind of church. Churches, especially those that have a long history, possess corporate cultures that have deep roots. It can be a monumental challenge to make the transition from a primary concern for keeping members and maintaining the status quo to a more outward missional focus. Leaders who take on such a transition need strong personal spirituality, well-honed leadership skills, and patience with parishioners who have the courage to step into a new journey, toward the heart of God. Those leaders can—indeed must—be both clergy and laity. It is for you who can become such leaders that *Shaped by God's Heart* is written.

As a student of God and His church, it is my privilege to handle profoundly Holy things. With humility I offer these pages in gratitude to our missional God and His missional church.

PART ONE

THE CHURCH
IN A NEW AND
CHANGING WORLD

But thanks be to God, who always leads us
in His triumph in Christ, and manifests
through us the sweet aroma of the
knowledge of Him in every place.

—2 Corinthians 3:14

ON SEPTEMBER 8, 2001, outfitter and wilderness guide Don
Wade and a client packed gear into the small float plane of
pilot Buck Maxen, stationed at Kotzebue. This was the third
aircraft into which Don had transferred the gear since leaving his Texas base for Northern Alaska. The craft would land
on a small lake near the Selawik River, just beneath the Arc-
tic Circle. From there Don would guide his client in a challenging trek through some of the most pristine and unspoiled
terrain in North America. Without radios or satellite phones,
he would be responsible for ensuring the safe and timely ren-
dezvous of his expedition with the pilot thirty miles downriver and fifteen days later. He had filed the drop-off and

pickup locations with the Alaska Fish and Game Department. They were the only documentation of his intended itinerary.

It took two full days to transport the gear from the small lake to the river less than a mile away. Because of the ubiquitous marshlands, Don and his client lived in hip boots for fifteen days. With every step, feet sank up to ankles in mud. Nights proved threatening, with temperatures that could plunge as low as sixty degrees below zero. Each day the absolute quiet of the undisturbed environment, the bounty of nature, and the evening meal of fish taken moments earlier from the river, rekindled Don's appreciation of his precarious position in the world.

Late each evening he thought of his family, thousands of miles away, and prayed all was well with them. Then, weary from his responsibilities, he would doze off. The next morning he would make coffee and hot cereal before breaking camp and continuing downriver. Each night, he would lie down again and fall into deep sleep.

On the morning of September 11, 2001, he was preparing hot cereal in the pristine and timeless wilderness, while those of us with access to radio and television were witnessing, over and over again, the horror of commercial airliners flying into the Pentagon and the twin towers of the World Trade Center, destroying the lives of thousands of people, and changing our own lives forever.

For Don—oblivious to the tragedy that rocked the nation, and to the heightened security that grounded all planes for three days—September 11 was simply day four of a journey down the Selawik River. It was another day to guide his client and enjoy the beauty of Alaskan wilderness. It was another night to lie down and wonder about family and friends, remembering them in darkness.

On September 21, Buck Maxen's plane circled another small lake and then landed to begin the process of retrieving Don and his client. As the propellers stopped turning, Buck stepped out and began telling them about the events of September 11. That night, Don was alone for one more night, as Buck continued the long process of removing the client and his gear. Don lay awake, trying without success to grasp the reality of what had happened to the world.

While Don was away in the harsh beauty of the natural world, our world had changed. The change was so dramatic that his isolation from the world's reality made it almost impossible for him to comprehend.

———————— o ————————

Don Wade's experience may seem extreme, but it has much in common with the situation in which many of our churches now find themselves.

Born into an ordered world of accepted rules and expected outcomes, enjoying many years of success and sameness, they suddenly find themselves with little that is familiar, to sustain them in a world that seems to have changed overnight.

Today, while the U.S. population soars, the percentage of those who hold membership in the Christian church continues to decline. Yet people still seek answers to deep questions of the soul, answers to the "Why?" of existence. As our traditional idea of church seems to be losing ground, a new and still forming movement—that of the missional church—seems to understand not only how to respond to these eternal questions but also how to ride out the waves of a changing culture.

You may find missional churches hard to identify. Some look very traditional, with church buildings and stratified leadership and social groups. Others look very untraditional—perhaps meeting in homes, or in community venues, in bars after hours, ministering to people on the margins, acting on "radical" ideas. Still others combine both ways of being in the world. New movements are by nature chaotic, ever-growing, and changing. The same can be said of missional churches. Yet the passion, commitment, and sheer aliveness of these churches draws us to them again and again as the new harbingers of Christianity in this brave new millennium. In the first chapters of this book, we'll take a look at how the world is changing, and how missional churches are responding to the challenge.

FROM MAINTENANCE TO MISSIONAL

THE CHURCH IN A WORLD OF CHANGE

And just as we have borne the image of the earthly,
we shall also bear the image of the heavenly.

—1 Corinthians 15:49

We face a choice to be worldly Christians or world Christians.

—Paul Borthwick, *A Mind for Missions*

THE PROTESTANT CHURCH in North America was born into a comfortable and familiar environment that was favorable and respectful of its presence. For many years, new churches enjoyed the luxury of acceptance and power. They enjoyed what George Hunter called a "home-court advantage."

While enjoying the beauty of their religious experience, however, they became increasingly isolated from the world. Some were adamant exponents of this separation, citing such biblical admonitions as "Come out from among them and be separate" (2 Corinthians 6:17). They enjoyed being with their group on a spiritual journey and sought to add others along the way—especially those who were comfortable in the church environment. Over the years, this separation encouraged members to adopt a specialized language. In some churches, the phrase "She walked the aisle" indicates coming to faith. In other communities church members call others "Brother" or "Sister" even though they are unrelated. Unless one is familiar with the intent, being asked to "give your heart to Jesus" might sound like a request for organ donation! Active members learned such churchspeak as natives of the culture. Inevitably, perhaps, their relationships were primarily with other members of their faith family, and their activities increasingly involved these people with whom they held much in common. They thrived.

By the middle of the twentieth century, however, this relatively peaceful existence was beginning to fracture. The times were changing, and changing fast. Young people, once relatively obedient to their elders, found themselves in an exciting new teen culture. Television, radio, and newspapers communicated startling world events with an immediacy that brought the brutalities of war right into the living room. Violent and nonviolent protests challenged national interests. Social balance was upset. What was once considered right was now wrong; what was once considered blasphemy was commonplace. Graphic sexuality found its way onto movie screens. Risqué language crept into television programming. Challenges were met with claims of First Amendment freedoms.

As divorce and cohabitation became more commonplace, traditional family units seemed the exception rather than the rule. Racial and linguistic diversity was accompanied by growth in non-Christian religions. Many felt uncomfortable with mosques and temples constructed in their communities. Court cases challenged prayer in public schools, the Ten Commandments on courtroom walls, "so help me God" in courtroom oaths, "one nation under God" in the pledge of allegiance, and "in God we trust" on U.S. currency. Litigants sought to erase all evidence of Christian bias. It seemed like the end of the world for members of many Protestant churches. To some degree, it was.

Fighting Change with Maintenance

For many church members and leaders alike, these events seemed beyond comprehension. Impossible. Unreal. Even if they tried, they felt incapable of relating in the changing environment. Some longed to engage the changing culture and share with those who had never experienced the serenity and peace found in relationship with God and the members of His church, but to their surprise other people did not seem to see their church in the same way. They felt bewildered and under fire. In response, they retreated to the sanctuary, their place of comfort, growing ever more inward in their orientation. They maintained the status quo.

Not surprisingly, they found themselves increasingly out of touch with the rapids of cultural change and the real world in which their neighbors lived. Most cared about those on the outside, but they felt impotent to connect and share with unchurched persons in any significant way. Consequently, their churches no longer anticipated having a major impact upon society and hoped only to reach enough people to help the church survive. I call this prevalent consumer orientation, isolation from society, and associated lack of belief in capacity to have significant influence a *maintenance mentality*.

The culture in which the church exists is a changing river, charting its own path without regard to the preferences of previous generational or cultural systems. Members of today's churches, who once felt that they held the high ground in a vast Christian nation, now feel cut off and isolated—islands in a fast-flowing stream. Clearly, the Christian church in North America no longer possesses a home-court advantage.

Where, now, *is* our home? As more and more people live their lives in their cars, and constant migration from town to town and even country to country becomes commonplace, communities have naturally become less cohesive. Churches, once perceived as the center of community life, have become progressively irrelevant in increasingly diverse communities. Many people are clearly still interested in spirituality, as witnessed by the growing interest in Eastern and Native American religions, contemplative and monastic environments, holistic health, and nontraditional expressions of connection with the environment. Yet the percentage of the population practicing their faith within local churches continues to decline.

Given this situation, it's not surprising that many Western churches are now focused mostly on survival. These churches are no longer storming the gates of hell. They are simply trying to outlast the onslaught of secularism that threatens their existence. These churches are filled with members who have adopted and adapted to consumer culture. Just as they count on Wal-Mart meeting their material needs, they expect their churches to provide religious goods and services. Many of their pastors, like John, are struggling to hang on and give them access to a strong spiritual life.

Still, a change is on the horizon. Some churches—a relative few, but growing in strength and number—are beginning to understand that the key to a revived spirit is both to focus inward and also to move outward—

into the world. They see the future as one of bringing the Gospel alive for a new generation in a new world—so the church will not just survive, but thrive. These congregations focus on God's mission, *missio dei*. These *missional* churches—reproducing communities of authentic disciples, being equipped as missionaries sent by God, to live and proclaim His Kingdom in their world—have connected the pervasive hunger for spirituality with the ancient but contemporary invitation to know God and live to His glory. Jamye Miller, pastor of Christ Fellowship in Grapevine, Texas, sees missional churches as "life-giving, image bearing, reproducing, multiplying, Christ-manifesting churches that glorify Him."[1] Beyond focusing on maintenance or survival, they are energized as they reconnect with God and His mission.

Theological Foundations of Missional Churches

The Bible reveals that people are created for relationship with God for specific purposes. Foundationally, individuals are created to reflect the image of God, or *imago dei* (Genesis 1:26–27; 1 Corinthians 15:49; Romans 8:29; 2 Corinthians 3:18). (I encourage you to go to the Reflection and Application section at the end of the chapter and ponder these Scriptural passages, which are printed there in entirety.)

The intent of God has not changed with the passage of time. We are still created to reveal the image of God, as was His design before we yielded to temptations of sin. Subsequently, as those redeemed from sin, God desires His image to be imprinted upon His followers. They are to live as He lives, love what He loves, and pursue that which is on His heart. His church is to bear His image to a world that has not seen Him. The New Testament "Body" metaphor evidences God's purpose that His church reflect His image, as His Body being present in the world.

In His image, the Body of Christ will seek to accomplish His purpose. Those who bear His image are sent to serve His mission, *missio dei,* in the same way that Christ was sent to accomplish the Father's purpose. Many have found it instructive to simply reflect upon His statements recorded in the Gospel of John. Consider His dependence upon the Father, commitment to the Father's mission, and His indication of your continued pursuit of His purpose in several verses (John 4:34; 5:30; 6:38; 7:29; 8:29; 9:4; 12:49; 13:20; 17:3, 18; 20:21). (These passages too are printed in entirety in the Reflection and Application sections.) Christ's profound sense of commitment to the purpose for which He was sent resonates with clarity. His incarnational purpose was to accomplish His Father's will. Singular in focus, He knew His purpose. Just as certainly, He indicated the purpose for His followers. They are to continue pursuing His purpose. God's mission, Jesus' mission, is the mission of His church.

A final end toward which the church is sent as image bearer of God remains. Ultimately, His church exists for the glory of God, *gloria dei.* Jealous for His own glory, this perfect, righteous, loving deity is unwilling to share His glory with another (1 Chronicles 16: 24, 29; Isaiah 43:1,7; Matthew 5:16; Ephesians 1:5–6, 12–14. Again, see the Reflection and Application sections for the full text.)

God desires His church to relish in His glory, share His glory among the nations, and reflect His glory in word and deed. The church is a Body made in His image, sent on His mission, to be to His glory!

A Change Agent Adept at Change

A church sent into an ever-changing environment must be fluid in its capacity to adapt while maintaining a clear commitment to its unchanging purpose and God's eternal truth. Jesus assigned His mission to a Body with adaptive ability, not to a rigid organization. Churches must continuously retool themselves for effectiveness in communicating the message of hope in the rapids of changing cultures. Today, however, most churches struggle with change. As one church leader said, "Churches are very willing to change. They will make any change necessary to keep things the same!"

Change is difficult, and deep culture change is especially hard. Most churches are structured for continuity of what they have been in an age of Christendom, rather than being change, ready to accomplish mission in today's culture. Darrell Guder, editor and contributing author of *Missional Church: A Vision for the Sending of the Church in North America,* describes this as the "museum curator" mentality found in many churches. This mentality focuses on "preserving the 'savedness' of the members, and the church's function to manage that salvation."[2]

Bishop Claude E. Payne offers an extensive and excellent distinction regarding churches focused on maintenance in contrast to mission. He says that two tensions are present in churches: creating community among members and reaching those who are not members. "Today's maintenance-centered Church ministers primarily to the faithful . . . It is not particularly attentive to the unchurched except philosophically, paying only lip service to the idea of evangelism. In the maintenance church, both clergy and laity lose sight of their obligation to make disciples."[3]

Most observers would agree that Christendom is over, if it really ever existed. Societal changes force the church to carry out its mission in an environment more like that in which the first-century church was born than perhaps any subsequent period in history. In this environment, the church is challenged to participate with God in His redemptive activity. As a missional community, the church expresses the incarnational reality of Christ, present and ministering in the world. At its core, all mission is incarnational. As Michael Riddell says, "Participating in the mission of God means leaving our place of security, to travel to the place where others are. This is the heartbeat of the incarnation. . . . Mission is always in the direction of the other, and away from ourselves."[4]

Missional churches exist as the presence of Christ, those who know Him and make Him known to others. Knowing Him transforms the lifestyle of His followers, those who are being equipped to live as authentic disciples. They are each being shaped by God's heart, conformed to His will, committed to His mission. As Jimmy Seibert of Antioch Community Church in Waco, Texas, told me, "We have a passion for Jesus and His purpose in the earth."[5]

Mission-Minded or Missional?

If you are confused by the term *missional church,* you are not alone—it's so new that most Christians are still coming to terms with it. In fact, if you search the pages of books written before the 1990s, you will not find the word *missional.* No dictionary included the word; most still do not. In 1991, Charles Van Engen first referred to "missional relationships" as he addressed the role of the local church in the world. Explaining his intent in using the word, Van Engen recently wrote to me, "When I began using the term, I was not aware of anyone else using it yet. I meant a quality of the essence of being Church."[6]

Some insist the term *missional church* is redundant, like "canine dog" or "feline cat." In fact, it is not. All dogs may be canine and all cats feline, but not all churches are missional. Many leaders who hear "missional church" respond that theirs is a very mission-minded church, assuming the terms to be synonymous. As you will see in this book, they are not. Much of the mission enterprise of Western churches has been enabled by mission-minded churches. Such churches view their role as sending and supporting those who have been "called" to mission service. "Mission" is therefore representative; church members pray and give so that others may go and serve. Just as churches have other programs, such as Christian Education and choral music, they also have a missions program. The word *missions* is but one expression of the church.

People in the missional church do pray and give so that others may go and serve; yet for them *missions* is more centered in "being and doing" than "sending and supporting." The missional church understands that although some may be supported as those sent to other locations, every member of the church is "sent." Mission is therefore participative rather than simply representative.

In this sense, *every member is a missionary. Missions* is not perceived as an expression of the missional church, but as the essence of the church. Pastor Nilson Fanini of First Baptist Church of Niterói, Brazil, communicates this vision simply: "Missions is our mission."[7] The church he pastors sponsors a school, a missionary training center, and a seminary to equip leaders for missional churches; it offers more than one hundred community ministries. The church has missionaries serving around the world.

We can break down the difference between a mission-minded church and a missional church as follows:

- The mission-minded church emphasizes *sending and supporting;* the missional church emphasizes *being and doing.*

- The mission-minded church is *representative;* the missional church is *participative.*

- The mission-minded church perceives mission as *one expression of its ministry;* the missional church perceives mission as *the essence of its existence.*

The rest of this book explores the nature of missional churches, the practices that separate them from traditional churches, and structures and strategies for becoming missional.

Becoming Missional

Can a mission-minded church become a missional church? Emphatically, yes. The key for contemporary churches that want to be counterculture agents for spiritual transformation is to move beyond maintenance, reconnecting with God's purpose for His church.

As author John Steinbeck was preparing to embark on a journey across the United States, he described the nature of a trip with these words: "We find after years of struggle that we do not take a trip; a trip takes us."[8] Missional churches understand that sentiment. They have not chosen God's mission; God has chosen them for His missional purpose. The initiative for mission lies in God. Jesus said, "You did not choose Me, but I chose you, and appointed you, that you should go and bear fruit, and that your fruit should remain; that whatever you ask of the Father in my name,

He may give to you" (John 15:16). The impetus for mission resides in Christ, who invites the church to become His missional Body.

A missional church is a reproducing community of authentic disciples, being equipped as missionaries sent by God, to live and proclaim His Kingdom in their world. The community does not own the mission; they are, however, invited to share its marvelous wonder. Missional churches and their disciples may be like the son in Henry Van Dyke's pleasant treatise *Who Owns the Mountains?* While enjoying the beauty of a mountain range, the young son asked his father, "Who owns the mountains?" only to be told of their impending sale to a logging company. After a quiet moment of reflection, the child remarked with simple profundity, "Well, I don't see what difference that makes. Everybody can look at them." Of the mountains, Van Dyke later said, "We knew and loved them all; they ministered peace and joy to us; they were all ours, though we held no title deed and our ownership had never been recorded."[9]

The missional church holds no title deed to God's mission, but it enjoys witnessing the beauty of God's handiwork as, through His church, God invites people to be transformed by the dynamic Gospel of grace and love. To the incipient missional church, Christ said, "You shall receive power when the Holy Spirit has come upon you; and you shall be My witnesses both in Jerusalem, and in all Judea and Samaria, and even to the remotest part of the earth" (Acts 1:8).

It is His mission. It is His missional church. In the next chapter, we look at how this church moves outward to bring its passion for God into the world.

Reflection and Application

1. Please take some time to reflect on these biblical passages, which were referenced in this chapter. Let God speak to you as one who is created in His image, to live His mission, that He will receive glory.

IMAGE OF GOD (*IMAGO DEI*)
Then God said, "Let Us make man in Our image, according to Our likeness. . . ." And God created man in His own image, in the image of God He created him; male and female He created them. (Genesis 1:26–27)

And just as we have borne the image of the earthly, we shall also bear the image of the heavenly. (1 Corinthians 15:49)

For whom He foreknew, He also predestined to become conformed to the image of His Son, that He might be the first-born among many brethren. (Romans 8:29)

But we all, with unveiled face beholding as in a mirror the glory of the Lord, are being transformed into the same image from glory to glory, just as from the Lord, the Spirit. (2 Corinthians 3:18)

MISSION OF GOD (*MISSIO DEI*)
Jesus said to them, "My food is to do the will of Him who *sent* me, and to accomplish His work." (John 4:34)

I can do nothing on My own initiative. As I hear, I judge; and My judgment is just, because I do not seek My own will, but the will of Him who *sent* Me. (John 5:30)

For I have come down from heaven, not to do my own will, but the will of Him who *sent* Me. (John 6:38)

I know Him; because I am from Him, and He *sent* Me. (John 7:29)

And He who *sent* Me is with Me; He has not left Me alone, for I always do the things that are pleasing to Him. (John 8:29)

We must work the works of Him who *sent* Me, as long as it is day; night is coming, when no man can work. (John 9:4)

And Jesus cried out and said, "He who believes in Me does not believe in Me, but in Him who *sent* Me. And he who beholds Me beholds the One who *sent* Me." (John 12:44–45)

For I did not speak on My own initiative, but the Father Himself who *sent* Me has given Me commandment, what to say, and what to speak. (John 12:49)

Truly, truly, I say to you, he who receives whomever I *send* receives Me; and he who receives Me receives Him who *sent* Me. (John 13:20)

And this is eternal life, that they may know Thee, the only true God, and Jesus Christ whom Thou hast *sent*. (John 17:3)

For the words which Thou gavest Me I have given to them; and they received them, and truly understood that I came forth from Thee, and they believed that Thou didst *send* Me. (John 17:8)

As Thou didst *send* Me into the world, I also have *sent* them into the world. (John 17:18)

Jesus therefore said to them again, "Peace be with you; as the Father has *sent* Me, I also *send* you." (John 20:21)

GLORY OF GOD (*GLORIA DEI*)

Tell of His *glory* among the nations, His wonderful deeds among all the peoples. Ascribe to the Lord the *glory* due to His name; bring an offering and come before Him; worship the Lord in holy array. (1 Chronicles 16: 24, 29)

But now, thus says the Lord, your creator, O Jacob, and He who formed you, O Israel, "Do not fear, for I have redeemed you; I have called you by name; You are Mine! Every one who is called by My name, and whom I have created for My *glory*, whom I have formed even whom I have made." (Isaiah 43:1, 7)

Let your light shine before men in such a way that they may see your good works, and *glorify* your Father who is in heaven. (Matthew 5:16)

He predestined us to adoption as sons through Jesus Christ to Himself, according to the kind intention of His will, to the praise of the *glory* of His grace, which He freely bestowed on us in the Beloved. To the end that we who were the first to hope in Christ should be to the praise of His *glory*. In Him, you also, after listening to the message of truth, the gospel of your salvation—having also believed, you were sealed in Him with the Holy Spirit of promise, who is given as a pledge of our inheritance, with a view to the redemption of God's own possession, to the praise of His *glory*. (Ephesians 1:5–6, 12–14)

2. Michael Riddell said, "Mission is not an optional extra for the church."[10]

- What do you think he means?
- How does this meaning apply to your church?

3. Compare the culture in which your church was founded with its current cultural context. How have "being" and "doing" changed from then to now? Identify five of these changes that best indicate your church's capacity to adapt effectively in a changing culture.

4. For this exercise, enlist six members of your congregation—preferably two newer members, two older members, at least one youth, and one young adult. Ask them to respond to these questions, and then compare their responses.

- How does our church help you be transformed into the image of Christ?

- Through which means does our church prepare you to carry out God's mission?
- How does our church best glorify God?

Now, propose strategies to strengthen members' expression of each area of theological foundation.

5. In a small-group setting, brainstorm how disciples can:

- Transfer their learning, skills, insights, and values into the world
- Bring experiences and skills from the world into the church

SUGGESTED READING

Van Gelder, C. *The Essence of the Church: A Community Created by the Spirit.* Grand Rapids, Mich.: Baker Books, 2000.

2

BE CHURCH AND BE CHANGED

HOW MISSIONAL CHURCHES LIVE THEIR PASSION

And Jesus answered and said to him, "It is written, 'You shall worship the Lord your God and serve Him only.'"

—Luke 4:8

Knowing where you're going is the first step to getting there.

—Ken Blanchard, *We Are the Beloved*

"IF WE HAVE NO POWER, the emerging cultures will not be drawn to us. They are not afraid they are going to go to church and be changed. They are more afraid they will go to church and *not be changed*."

With these words to a gathering of church leaders, Shannon Hopkins, a young visionary with Emerging Church Network, captured the essence of missional churches: they are not content simply to take up space in the community. They understand that Christ initiated His church as a movement, with the big idea of inviting all people to experience life-transforming relationship with Jesus Christ. "And this is the real and eternal life: 'That they know you, the one and only true God, and Jesus Christ, whom you sent'" (John 17:3, *The Message*).

Most of us would say that, individually, we feel passionate about God. Many of us would also say that we feel passionate about our church. But for missional churches, the passion does not stay personal or referential; it is the essence of and expression of their corporate culture, the primary value that drives their behavior. Missional churches are not just there on Sunday; they are determined to bring the transformational influence of Jesus Christ into their world every day.

The Four Dimensions of Missional Churches

If you observe missional churches for any length of time, you begin to see that what drives them is a unified passion expressed through four dimensions (Figure 2.1):

Dimension One: Love God

Dimension Two: Live His mission

Dimension Three: Love people

Dimension Four: Lead them to follow

Let's take a moment to look at how these dimensions work.

Missional Dimension One: Love God

Connie Wilson, of United Methodist Church of the Resurrection in Leawood, Kansas, says, "People say when they walk into our church they feel something, and mostly what people experience is the presence of the Holy

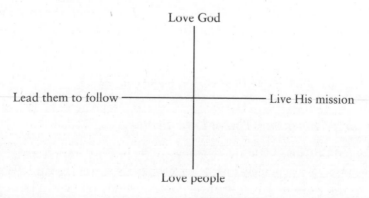

Figure 2.1. The Four Missional Dimensions.

Spirit. People coming to our church are seekers, so they do not know how to name it. They often refer to an energy or warmth that they can connect with. What they don't know is they are experiencing our deep love relationship with God and His presence among our people."[1] I heard about—and witnessed—this intangible but real difference in the quality of their love for God over and over again in missional churches the world over.

Members of missional churches love God not as a distant father, but as One with whom they have intimate relationship. They do not simply know about God; they know Him. To know Him is to love Him. They have responded, with Jesus' answer, to the question, "What is the greatest commandment?" He said, "Love the Lord your God with all your heart and with all your soul and with all your mind" (Matthew 22:37 NIV).

Missional Dimension Two: Live His Mission

Missional churches sense God's love for all the nations of the earth. They are driven by His love to live His mission every day. Indeed, they understand His mission to be the reason for which they exist. They have responded not only to Jesus' great commandment but also to His great commission: "Then Jesus came and said to them, 'All authority in heaven and on earth has been given to me. Therefore go and make disciples of all nations, baptizing them in the name of the Father and of the Son and of the Holy Spirit, teaching them to obey everything I have commanded you. And surely I am with you always, to the very end of the age'" (Matthew 28:18–20 NIV).

Missional churches take this mandate seriously. As one pastor said with a laugh, "It is not called the Great *Suggestion*." Dayton and Fraser address the church's appropriate response to God's mission in *Planning Strategies for World Evangelization*: "When the church ceases to reach out to all people, it ceases to be a true church. This is why the Great Commission is a controlling and central command. All these metaphors and commands spring out of one profound reality: *the church is a result of and a participant in the mission of God*."[2] J. Andrew Kirk calls the church's participation in mission essential, a self-defining reality: "The Church is by nature missionary to the extent that, if it ceases to be missionary, it has not just failed in one of its tasks, it has ceased being Church."[3]

Missional Dimension Three: Love People

Missional Christians find that as they are shaped by God's heart, objects of His love, they genuinely love other people. Experiencing His love motivates them to fulfill the rest of the Great Commandment, "Love your neighbor as yourself'" (Matthew 22:39 NIV). This command knows no limitations. Missional churches do not choose whom they will love.

Matt Hannan, pastor of New Heights Church in Vancouver, Washington, told me about his church's acceptance of and ministry among chemically dependent persons. The ministry began with a twelve-step study for a small group of church members and their friends. As the group grew and participants continued inviting others, Matt felt it appropriate to offer the ministry as a series in evening services. When he asked the group how they felt about this idea, they responded positively. So he approached the elders and leaders, saying, "Let's do it for the whole church." With their agreement, the church began to spread the word: "If you or someone you love fits this category, this is going to be helpful. You don't have to be addicted. You can come because you care for someone who struggles with chemical dependency."

The services grew to standing room only, and Matt said to those gathered, "If you are here and you struggle with addiction, if you are an alcoholic, you are battling a major issue. The good word I have for you is, 'Welcome home. You have found a church that wants to help you find victory.'"

Matt smiled as he shared a story of one of the church's elders. The man came to him after that first evening and said, "One of your best gifts of leadership is that you lie with love for people." He meant that Matt's declaration that those with addictions would be accepted issued a challenge to the congregation: they were to make the promised acceptance reality. Reflecting on that experience, Matt saw his actions as "just part of setting the corporate culture," which he sees as the larger leadership challenge. Whether or not members were ready to love, his confident statement confirming their acceptance meant it was as good as done.

One criterion that brands individuals as legitimate disciples of Christ is love. "By this will all men know that you are My disciples, if you have love for one another" (John 13:35). Members of missional churches love people without reservation. They love God, live His mission, and love people.

Missional Dimension Four: Lead Them to Follow

Missional churches are not content simply to love people; they desire to see every person become an authentic disciple of Jesus Christ. They long to see them become those who will love God, live His mission, love people, and lead those who will to become followers . . . who will, in turn, love God . . . and on and on and on.

The circle is completed and begins again. It is centrifugal force, pushing outward to others. All too often, our churches seem to operate by centripetal force—pulling everything to the inside, their existence revolving around themselves. Missional churches, those on mission with God, focus beyond themselves to love people and lead them into authentic discipleship. Their vision is the multiplication of missional churches and the continued outward spin of the encompassing love of God among all the nations of the earth. Jimmy Seibert, pastor of Antioch Community Church in Waco, told me, "Our goal is not to get people 'in' our church, our goal is to equip people to go out from our church. We are here to equip them to be ready for God's mission, anywhere in the world. Our task is to enable disciples who can instantly respond to God's direction."

The Eight Passion Actions

Living these four dimensions creates a perpetual cycle of passionate action that missional Christians strive to accomplish every day. Further, as Figure 2.2 illustrates, each missional dimension generates two passion actions. Together, they constitute the living passion of missional churches. As a model, it is an ever-encompassing system:

- Love God: worship and obey
- Live His mission: serve and share
- Love people: embrace and invite
- Lead them to follow: equip and empower

Figure 2.2. The Self-Perpetuating Cycle of Missional Churches.

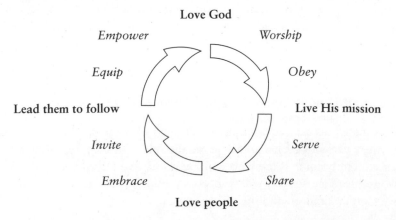

Their vision is that the new disciple will ultimately love God, live His mission, love people, and lead them to follow . . . as those who love God . . . The systemic cycle grows exponentially as missional communities live their passion.

Passion Action One—Love God: Worship

In missional churches worship is not expressed once a week on Sunday but is dynamic and constantly developing. It actively reflects a Body growing in intimacy and knowledge of its Lord. As the relationship deepens, so does the expression of worship.

Worship is the natural expression of adoration and obeisance from the heart that knows God's love. It is the appropriate response to relationship with Him. As objects of His love, missional Christians express their responding love for God through worship. The sacrifice He desires is the surrender of His followers to Himself. Through worship, disciples express praise to God who "inhabits the praise" of His people (Psalm 22:3).

Although all Christians should worship God, for missional churches worship is tied to mission. Knowing that God seeks those who will worship Him, they seek others who will join them in resounding praises to God through worship. Were everyone on earth to know God and offer Him praise, there would be no mission. In the words of John Piper, "Worship is the fuel of missions. . . . Missions exist because worship doesn't."[4]

Passion Action Two—Love God: Obey

Obedience is a logical response to God's love and the appropriate response to His revelation. As authentic disciples, missional Christians seek to live in obedience to His commands. God has indicated His pleasure in the obedience of His followers: "Has the Lord as much delight in burnt offerings and sacrifices as in obeying the voice of the Lord? Behold, to obey is better than sacrifice, and to heed than the fat of rams" (1 Samuel 15:22).

Obedience is another diagnostic indicator of authentic discipleship: "And by this we know that we have come to know Him, if we keep His commandments" (1 John 2:3). Missional Christians hold themselves and other members of the Body accountable for obedience. They are not satisfied simply to know the Word of God. Since God has revealed His purpose in the Bible, they seek to respond to its teachings in obedience. Missional Christians have no alternative.

Obedience involves surrender and trust. Missional communities trust God's faithfulness as they journey into the future. Because His faithfulness merits obedience, members commit to obey. They walk transparently among others as the way unfolds before them. They risk vulnerability with other believers as they corporately seek to follow Christ. For some, this aspect of the missional church is too dangerous. Perhaps they can trust *God* to be aware of their failures, but trusting other *people* is something else. Part of obedience is learning to trust. It is sharing failures and finding encouragement to try again among others who are themselves "walking naked into the land of uncertainty."

Speaking of the disciples' obedience, Joseph Stowell of Moody Bible College wrote: "His claim and call obviously resonated in their souls. So they followed Him into the face of uncertainty. . . . For followers, all the question marks fall into line behind Christ, who is the exclamation point."[5]

Passion Action Three—Live His Mission: Serve

Jesus inverted the cultural concept of greatness when he communicated His personal mission with His disciples. Jesus said, "But whoever wishes to become great among you shall be your servant, and whoever wishes to be first among you shall be your slave; just as the Son of Man did not come to be served, but to serve, and to give His life a ransom for many" (Matthew 20:26–28). He came to serve. Before His death he wrapped a towel around Himself and washed the feet of His band of disciples . . . the role of a servant. He called them to assume the same role, "I gave you an example that you also should do as I did to you" (John 13:15). No task was too small for Jesus. He came to serve.

Because missional churches live His mission, they place emphasis on serving and sharing. They are convinced of the mystical truth, "Truly I say to you, to the extent that you did it to one of these brothers of Mine, even the least of them, you did it to Me" (Matthew 25: 40). Through ministry they touch Christ. These communities of faith follow the leadership of Christ in providing compassionate care to persons in need; they offer extensive ministries to meet physical, social, mental, physical, and spiritual needs of people in their communities. They minister because they are the Body of Christ and consequently serve as He did. They know that ministry, even to the least, is ministry unto Christ (Matthew 25:40).

Passion Action Four—Live His Mission: Share

Missional churches also delight in sharing the motivation that moves them to minister. They are compelled to share the message of hope to which they have responded. They know that people are designed for relationship with God, and they sincerely believe the words of Saint Augustine: "Our souls find no rest, until they find their rest in Thee." Therefore, missional churches seek to minister to the spiritual need of those in their spheres of influence. Missional communities seek to live authentic lives as disciples of Jesus Christ and, in so doing, validate the transformational promise that God does change lives. As missional communities reflect the grace of Christ in their lives, they also share the availability of grace with others, creatively and clearly.

· Charles Wade, executive director of the Baptist General Convention of Texas, encourages churches to "be the presence of Christ" in their communities. This singular refrain calls churches to fulfill their incarnational purpose as the Body of Christ. His mission in the incarnation was to seek and to save that which was lost (Luke 19:10). As His Body, His incarnational presence, the missional church now assumes the same purpose.

This means the church is sent to accomplish the task of evangelization. Note the term *evangelization,* not simply evangelism. The latter is more often used of the declaration of the Gospel. The former, evangelization, includes both the declaration *and* the demonstration of the Gospel of Jesus Christ. It requires sharing and serving. This is the mission to which the church is committed.

Passion Action Five—Love People: Embrace

A number of years ago, a group of churches joined together to share God's heart with residents in the area of El Paso, Texas. As they sought a theme around which they could develop an identity as the Body of Christ, they adopted a Spanish phrase, *Abrazando El Paso.* Those churches were saying, "We are here to give El Paso a big hug!" What an appropriate phrase for the relationship offered through the Body of Christ.

Missional communities have experienced the love of Christ and are commanded by Him to share that love with others. To embrace is to extend arms of acceptance and compassion. It is the image of Christ reflected in Matthew 11:28, "Come to Me, all you who are weary and heavy laden, and I will give you rest." His love is unconditional and indiscriminate. His embrace is to "whoever will" (Revelation 22:17). As authentic disciples, missional Christians extend the loving embrace of Christ to those in their world.

This embrace also motivates missional churches to stand with those who cannot stand for themselves. Missional churches are motivated by Christ's concern for the poor, the disenfranchised, the helpless, and the homeless. The indiscriminate embrace of Christ motivates churches to become advocates for powerless persons in their communities. In this advocacy, missional churches seek the peace and righteousness of God, the *shalom* promised in the Old Testament.

Passion Action Six—Love People: Invite

Some who experience the loving embrace of Christ through His Body will desire to become part of the Body. As the missional church serves and shares, it both demonstrates the reality of Christ's love and invites others to experience His love personally. The authenticity of members of the missional community resonates as genuine among people who intuitively long for spiritual reality they have never consciously known.

Missional communities create multiple entry points through which the spiritual inquirer can begin the journey toward faith. In other words, missional churches are specialists at extending invitation. They invite people to begin walking with them toward Christ, well before those people may grasp what it means to become His disciple. They invite people to ask difficult questions about faith in God. Ultimately they invite spiritual searchers to become authentic disciples, members of the missional community.

Passion Action Seven—Lead Them to Follow: Equip

Many churches act as though their task is completed once someone has responded to their invitation. Once outsiders have become part of the church, the church's job with them is done; focus is directed toward reaching more outsiders. In missional communities, response to invitation is considered the beginning, not the end. When people respond to the invitation, becoming followers of Christ, the developmental task of leading them to maturity begins.

The New Testament term used to denote the process of development is "equipping." It acknowledges a major function of church leadership, "equipping of the saints for the work of service" (Ephesians 4:12). The local church is the primary training center in the development of Christians. Schools, colleges, universities, and seminaries have their own critical functions; the church has the assignment of equipping disciples to live as authentic followers of Christ. Equipping prepares all members of the Body to contribute their gifts and functions through which God accomplishes His missional purpose via the church.

Passion Action Eight—Lead Them to Follow: Empower

Ability without opportunity frustrates. Ultimately atrophy results if muscles remain dormant. Too many disciples have a long tenure of training without expressing through ministry the gifts and talents the Spirit has built into their lives. Missional communities not only equip members, *they equip members for something*. The purpose of equipping is ministry in God's mission.

Robert Lewis verbalized the profound impact ultimately resulting from a simple question posed to Fellowship Bible Church. Of their commitment to equip members, he wrote: "They had always been told that they were to be 'equipped,' but the data raised a greater question: 'Equipped *for what?*' In the history of our church, nothing has shocked us as much as that simple, three-word question. . . . one that would eventually lead to a complete reconstruction of Fellowship Bible Church."[6] As a result of that incendiary experience, Fellowship Bible Church developed processes that give as much attention to empowering members as to equipping members. Suddenly, the task of equipping had an energizing effect, as members were deployed in ministries through which their passion and equipping could produce Kingdom fruit.

Missional churches equip God's people to be on mission. They encourage and empower them. They enthusiastically believe in their ability to serve as God's missional people. Charles Van Engen reminds us of the implications found in the disciple's designation as salt. "The image of salt reminds us that an important aim must be to scatter or launch the saints. Unless they are the *missionary* people of God, they cannot be the salt *of the earth*."[7] When the church empowers, salt influences society and light dispels its darkness.

Practicing What We Preach

Clearly, "faith on Sunday, work on Monday" is not the credo of people in missional communities. They are driven to love God and share that love every day, in everything they do. The kind of action that moves outward from a strong core of faith drives their passion. This passion is reflected in nine practices, which we look at in depth in the next section.

As we move to investigate these nine practices, it is vital to remember that although practices can be imitated, passion cannot. Unless practices emerge out of a deep passion, they are little more than sound and fury—motion without effect. In this case, passion is kindled only in the midst of a white-hot love relationship with God. Knowing Him, His heart, yields passion. Pursuing what is on His heart informs practice.

Reflection and Application

1. Illustrate the self-perpetuating cycle of the passions of a missional church through this game:

• Divide members into four groups. Instruct each group to prepare a team charade for their assigned component of the passion of missional churches (Love God, Live His Mission, Love People, Lead Them to Follow). Allow time for teams to prepare and practice their charade in separate areas.

• Bring the four teams together and invite them to present their charade, one group at a time, as others attempt to solve the charade. After the first statement has been solved, proceed to the second group following the same procedure. Before going to the third group, allow group one to repeat their charade followed immediately by group two. As the charades are pantomimed, participants should say the phrase as well. Continue until all four groups have presented and all participants have verbalized the passion statements.

• To emphasize the cyclical nature of the passion, allow groups to present in consecutive order (group one: Love God, group two: Live His Mission, group three: Love People, group four: Lead those who will follow) with group one beginning again following group four. Allow a constant motion to flow, group to group, for at least three cycles.

2. Design your own method of illustrating the self-perpetuating cycle of the passions of a missional church.

3. Recall events and tell stories that illustrate your church's commitment to the Great Commission and the Great Commandment.

4. Review the passion actions discussed in this chapter. Is your church reflecting them passionately or just going through the motions?

Suggested Reading

Hanks, B., Jr. *A Call to Growth: Establishing the Growing Believer.* Nashville: Word Ministry Resources, 1993.

Harper, N. *Urban Churches: Vital Signs—Beyond Charity Toward Justice.* Grand Rapids, Mich.: Eerdmans, 1999.

Hill, E. V. *A Savior Worth Having.* Chicago: Moody Press, 2002.

PART TWO

THE NINE ESSENTIAL PRACTICES OF MISSIONAL CHURCHES

*Therefore, my beloved brethren, be steadfast,
immovable, always abounding in the work
of the Lord, knowing that your toil
is not in vain in the Lord.*

—1 Corinthians 15:58

LOCATING MISSIONAL CHURCHES is a challenging task. When I asked Lois Barrett, contributing author to *Missional Church,* to identify churches she perceived as missional, she said, "There are no perfect churches, and there are no truly missional churches. But there are many who are on the journey in an intentional way toward becoming that kind of church. They proclaim and are a sign of the Kingdom reign of God in the world."[1]

Across the United States, God's Spirit is inviting churches to become missional communities. A new generation of leaders is hungering to lead God's people to rewrite the nature of church, scripting their pattern after the first-century faith community. Those churches are both small and large. Some look similar to traditional churches; others are nontraditional. They are cell churches and house churches. Some are affiliated with traditional denominations. Others are independent. Some own properties and offer traditional programming. Others gather in rented facilities or homes, using the simplest of structures.

Whatever their appearance and style, missional churches do possess common characteristics. Perhaps the most basic characteristic of missional churches is that they consistently focus beyond their own survival as an entity and invite others in the journey toward the heart of God. Observation soon reveals other common practices. Nine such practices repeatedly surfaced in churches that have committed to the missional journey.

These culture practices are not exhaustive, nor are they exclusive to missional churches. Your own church may already incorporate some of them. The term *missional church* is relatively new, and there is still much to learn about these churches that determine to reflect God's heart in life and practice. As these churches seek to reclaim the memory of the church Christ intended, they will be known by their actions.

MISSIONAL PRACTICE NUMBER ONE

HAVE A HIGH THRESHOLD FOR MEMBERSHIP

---

*But to each one is given the manifestation
of the Spirit for the common good.*

—1 Corinthians 12:7

*He cannot have God for his Father who
refuses to have the church for his mother.*

—Augustine

AUTHENTIC DISCIPLESHIP is costly—it accepts responsibilities. In describing the path of those who would follow Him, Jesus chose difficult and challenging words: "If anyone comes to Me, and does not hate his own father and mother and wife and children and brothers and sisters, yes, and even his own life, he cannot be My disciple. Whoever does not carry his own cross and come after Me cannot be My disciple" (Luke 14:26–27). He went on to share parables of those who would build towers or go to war without first counting the costs required in those initiatives. Jesus placed the truth boldly in front of people so they could make informed decisions. In so doing He maintained a high threshold for His followers. This threshold weeded out some whose motivation for following was less than genuine love for Him.

Missional churches are high-threshold churches, and they clearly communicate the responsibilities of church membership. The term *membership* is not found in the New Testament in the way it is most often used, a designation of one's identification with a specific local church. However, the word is used by the Apostle Paul to denote the disciple's status in the Body of Christ. All who had come to know Christ were members of the Body. Their membership linked them organically with other members of the Body: "Now you are Christ's body, and individually members of it" (1 Corinthians 12:27). The implications of that membership were interdependence and acceptance of mutual care.

Alan J. Roxburgh sees the missional community as a bounded set of believers covenanted together to live and proclaim the reign of God, in the context of their communities. This community invites searchers—those who are investigating spiritual issues—to join with them in their journey as pilgrims on their way toward the ultimate reign of God. In this paradigm the purpose of the church is realized as members of the bounded set evidence transformed lives that encourage the searchers to become authentic disciples joining with the covenant community in serving God's missional purpose.[1]

These are the elements that express the missional churches' high threshold for membership:

- They are concerned for nominal church members.
- Membership is not casual.
- They are a unified community.
- The church has clear expectations for members.
- Members have clear expectations of the church.

They Are Concerned for Nominal Church Members

Relatively few churches in North America can be identified as possessing a high threshold for membership. In *The Continuing Conversion of the Church*, Darrell Guder says that "most mainline churches maintain what is, interestingly, called a 'low threshold' to church membership. It is more difficult to become a member of many service clubs than to join most

Protestant congregations."[2] Over an extended period of time, low-threshold membership expectations result in large numbers of members who maintain only a minimal relationship with the church. Others completely abandon active participation in the activities of their local congregations but still view themselves as members.

The idea of being a church member without having a vital connection to the body is foreign to scripture. Yet its pervasiveness has resulted in the designation "nominal membership." This has been a tragedy for the Western Christian faith community.[3] Pervasive in practice, and debilitating in affect, nominal Christianity has little impact on marginally connected members, while it weakens the corporate body. Genuine Christianity is a communal experience, not simply an individual one.[4]

A number of ministers of my acquaintance are concerned about the spiritual condition of adult sons and daughters of church members. Most once participated in activities of the church, and their names were at some time added to the church membership. But their lives now bear no evidence of personal relationship with God. They are not living in obedience to His commands. They do not exhibit love for His Body. There is no fruit of the Spirit of grace that can be observed. Upon sharing this concern with the parents, these ministers are shocked to hear them respond, defensively, "Oh, don't worry. He was once active in church," or "But she was confirmed," or "He was baptized when he was ten years old"—as though there were some spiritual security to be gained from that nominal relationship. There are certainly differing theological assumptions that might address this experience, but surely it should pose a concern to the Western church when masses of formerly active congregants have now withdrawn from any connection with the Body. One might consider the implications of this difficult passage: "They went out from us, but they were not really of us; for if they had been of us, they would have remained with us; but they went out, so that it would be shown that they all are not of us" (1 John 2:19). Certainly one measure of discipleship is continuation in the faith with the Body.

The missional church is concerned for the masses who have never had opportunity to hear the wonderful Good News of the Gospel of Christ. It must also be concerned for the more than ten million in North America who were once part of the church but now have no relationship with any local Body of believers. It is too easy for members to disappear from the radar screen of churches with low-threshold membership requirements. Low-threshold churches suffer from associated poor accountability among members.

Membership Is Not Casual

The world's understanding of membership is strongly influenced by other contexts in which membership is held. Cogent thinker and missional leader Mark Thames, applying principles of field anthropology, says that most people today "hold membership" in stores such as Blockbuster Video or Sam's Club. Inevitably, he says, people "bring their idea of membership to the church rather than carry the church's idea of membership into the world. . . . Members, the people on the inside, do as little as is required to be part and have the benefit. Non-members, those on the outside, do as much as required to share the benefit without becoming a member."[5] His comments might seem cynical, but his observations merit consideration, since membership carries a variety of implications in North America. Without clearly communicated meaning, consideration of church membership is likely to be filled with ambiguity for the individual who has no previous relationship with the church.

This is in part why the missional church chooses to be so clear in explaining the reasons for and expectations of membership. NorthWood Church for the Communities in Keller, Texas, like other missional churches, has developed a clear pathway to membership. The church staff holds a weekly meeting in which prospective members are introduced to the church's history, beliefs, purpose, and goals. They also have the opportunity to begin to explore the place where they might "plug in and be part" of the fellowship. It is also at this time that they hear the meaning and reason for membership. The pastor or other staff member explains, "The difference between 'attenders' and 'members' can be summed up in one word: commitment." Their *Pilgrim's Progress Guide* details the four reasons NorthWood Church believes membership matters:

1. *A biblical reason:* Christ is committed to the church. ". . . Christ loved the church, and He gave His life for it" (Ephesians 5:25).

2. *A cultural reason:* it is an antidote to our society. We live in an age where very few want to be committed to anything—a job, a marriage, our country. This attitude has produced a generation of "church shoppers and hoppers." Membership swims against the current of America's consumer religion. It is an unselfish decision. Commitment always builds character.

3. *A practical reason:* it defines who can be counted on. Every team must have a roster. Every school must have an enrollment. Every business has a payroll. Every army has an enlistment. Even our country takes a census and requires voter registration. Membership identifies our family.

4. *A personal reason:* it produces spiritual growth. The New Testament places a major emphasis on the need for Christians to be account-

able to each other for spiritual growth. You cannot be accountable if you're not committed to any specific church family.[6]

They Are a Unified Community

The missional church is a community of believers who trust in God and depend on one another. This goes against the general direction of Western society, which has long been concerned with individualism. We hear this ideal reflected all the time in such common expressions as "He is his own man," "She is a self-made leader," and "He picked himself up by his own bootstraps." Of course, none of them can actually be true. People need each other. No one can make it completely on his or her own. We are designed for relationships, and community is critical.

The missional church is a community, a composite of its many members. Each member is unique, gifted by God to allow his or her own contribution to the building up of the Body. Every member possesses something the rest of the Body needs. Without the contribution of each member, the Body would not be complete. Members are mutually interdependent. The will to sacrifice for the good of another is a reflection of the nature of God. It is best expressed in the incarnation. The missional church, seeking to be the presence of Christ, mirrors this self-sacrificing attitude. Individual preferences are relinquished to the need of the Body.

This does not mean that members never disagree. Every person brings his or her own thought process, a unique sense of appropriate direction and what should and should not be done, to the community. Bringing diverse personalities together to form a single identity is challenging. In this environment, rugged individualism—"my way or the highway"—must be relinquished to the decision of the group.

Membership in community means that all members bring their unique perspective to decision making. Missional community members share their individual perspective and then surrender personal desire to what members sense to be direction from the heart of God. Together, they share their concerns and convictions, and together they seek direction. Not all may totally support the decision, but they support the direction of the Body. Business leader Max De Pree believes accomplishment of any vision depends on the willingness of those involved, "whether they agree or not, [to] say, 'OK, I'm with you. I'm going to stay on the team. I accept this.'"[7] That is unity.

Missional churches are made up of members who are convinced God has invited their community to participate in His mission and that accomplishment of His mission requires their unity. A missional church is no stronger than the mutually supportive relationship found within its membership. The Body is the composite of its members.

The Church Has Clear Expectations for Members

One means of achieving unity in a missional community is to state clearly what is expected of members. Grace Point Church in San Antonio, Texas, for example, has championed this task by making sure that the responsibilities of membership are not hidden. They communicate these expectations in a variety of printed documents, on posters throughout the property, and on their Website. These materials are given to all prospective new members during "base camp," a one-time class for visitors interested in learning more about the church. The expectations are also examined in the "discovery class" required for all new members.

New members must sign and commit to faithfully pursue the "Grace Point G5 Covenant" (specific components of the covenant refer to structures and practices that are unique to Grace Point, such as the Impact Card and 360 Community; the meaning of these terms is explained in the process leading to membership):

1. The Grace Covenant . . . is a commitment to building relationships and living out the grace that God has appropriated to us by:
- Praying for those on my Impact Card that I know do not have a personal relationship with Jesus Christ

- Sharing a verbal witness of God's grace using my own salvation story when the opportunity presents itself

- Inviting my friends, neighbors, relatives and coworkers to church (Ephesians 2:8–10, Matthew 28:19–20)

2. The Growth Covenant . . . is a commitment to pursue spiritual worth in a 360 Community through:
- Bible study

- Fellowship with other believers in my 360 Community

- Pursuing 360 relationships (Acts 2:42)

3. The Gift Covenant . . . is a commitment to discovering and using my God given gifts and abilities in serving God and others. I will strive to discover, based on my SHAPE [see Chapter Five], the right place of service on a Grace Point servant team (Ephesians 4:11–13).

4. The Give Covenant . . . is a commitment to be a responsible caretaker of the material resources that God has entrusted to me.

Understanding that everything belongs to God I commit to offering a tangible expression of my love for God by giving to the church:

- Systematically

- Sacrificially

- Proportionately (2 Corinthians 9:6–9)

5. The Go Covenant . . . is a commitment to take the message of God's love and grace to people all around the world. I commit to be involved in at least one:

- Local mission opportunity every year

- Global mission trip within the next five years (Acts 1:8, Matthew 28:19–20)

The Mosaic community, in Los Angeles, provides a "Partner's Check List" as a process guide for those considering membership. The list prompts prospective members in areas that are required for membership. Mosaic's Partner's Check List includes:

- Focused commitment to Jesus Christ

- Public confession of faith through baptism by immersion

- Connection to a Life Group

- Completion of "Mosaic Life in Christ" (five sessions)

- Completion of "Mosaic Life in Church" (one-day seminar)

- Embracing the "Partnership Covenant"

Mosaic, like other missional churches, communicates a pathway through which those who would become members can find their way into the community. Again, members are invited to evidence their commitment to the Mosaic community through a covenant. With the Mosaic Partnership Covenant, the individual is asked:

- To invest your passions (1 Thessalonians 5:4–28; Galatians 5:24–25) Honor God by following Christ personally and passionately. Your reputation is Christ's reputation and the church's reputation.

- To invest your service (Hebrews 10:23–25; Galatians 5:13) Participate in the life of the congregation through genuine worship, sharing, learning and serving.

- To invest your resources (1 Corinthians 16:2; 2 Corinthians 9:6–15) Support the gospel here and worldwide by tithing (10 percent of your income) and then by giving more as the Lord leads. Invest your time, skills, talents, and gifts in and through the church.

- To invest your relationships (Luke 10:25–37; Matthew 28:19–20) Develop authentic loving relationships with others in the church and establish significant relationships with those who do not know Jesus.[8]

Some maintenance churches do offer new-member orientation, but relatively few consistently communicate a pathway to learn more about the church and implications of membership. Missional churches provide both the pathway and the expectations of membership with consistency and excellence. If you are considering membership at United Methodist Church of the Resurrection in Leawood, Kansas, for example, you receive a worship folder and announcement guide inviting you to a "coffee with the pastor" session. The invitation explains, "At the coffee you'll learn more about the church, get to know our pastors and staff, and review expectations regarding membership. You will be given an opportunity to become a member of Church of the Resurrection in a brief ceremony following the information meeting."

If you visit New Heights Church in Vancouver, Washington, and wonder how you might join this church, a greeter (perhaps casually dressed in a golf shirt bearing the church's logo) gives you a full-page "Welcome." On that welcome page you read:

> If this is your first time at New Heights we're very glad you're here! Relax . . . we won't embarrass you or ask for money! We hope to give you something today—an enjoyable church experience that brings you closer to God. We do ask that you fill out the enclosed Communication Card so we can get to know you better and let us know how we can help you. Listed throughout this folder are lots of opportunities to encourage you on your spiritual journey. You'll find others there that can relate to you and your life and you'll probably have fun, too. Try one out!

In case you are interested in membership:

> Are you a newcomer or been around for a while but still have questions about New Heights? You don't need a secret decoder ring to figure this place out! Come to New Heights 101, a class designed just for you. Join us Saturday, 7:00 P.M. in room 112 or Sunday, 9:45 A.M. in room 103. This is also the first step toward church membership if you're interested (no obligation). Just show up! We'd love to have you.

At Fellowship Bible Church in Little Rock, Arkansas, you will be invited to Discovery I, an informal two-and-a-half-hour meeting that provides information about the church's ministries, beliefs, and other helpful resources as well as an opportunity to visit with church leaders. At Christ Church Episcopal in Overland Park, Kansas, an invitation to the next "Alpha" course is placed in your hand as a guest. In their own way, each of these missional communities seeks to make the pathway to member-ship clear, inviting, and meaningful.

As with the pathway, they also clearly communicate the requirements of membership. Antioch Community Church presents this list of require-ments for new members:

- Has made a commitment to follow Christ
- Has been water baptized since becoming a Christian
- Has been attending a Lifegroup and Sunday Celebration Service
- Has read the summarized bylaws and agrees to follow the leader-ship of the church in matters of conduct and doctrine
- Has completed the membership course Antioch: Vision and Values
- Has completed and turned in a written membership form to Antioch Community Church
- Has completed a brief interview with the individual's Lifegroup leader

These requirements do not discourage. In fact, each of these missional churches is adding committed new members regularly. Their clearly stated pathway to membership, and its responsibilities, seems to add value to the meaning of membership for those who unite with these communities.

Members Have Clear Expectations of the Church

Consumers are accustomed to receiving lists of member benefits routinely accompanying marketing efforts. Church membership *does* have its bene-fits. So creative church communicators include "What's in it for me?" lists. The added values noted involve issues of much greater significance than free parking or child care. For example, members of Grace Point can expect:

1. To encounter God

    Through loving people

    Through vibrant worship

    Through interaction with God's Word

2. To be cared for by people you can trust

    Through quality child care (birth through three years)

    Through 360 Communities (Bible Studies)

3. To get connected with benefits of joining the journey

> You will be able to *effectively and graciously communicate Christ* to those you love and desire to see fully devoted to God.

> You will be able to *establish long-term and lasting relationships* that will help you grow closer to Christ and other people.

> You will *realize your unique purpose,* your God-given gifts, and discover the joy of serving in community.

> You will *discover God's timeless financial principles* and realize tangible and eternal return on your investments.

> You will forever *be changed as you go locally and globally* with the transforming message of Jesus Christ.

If membership can deliver those benefits, it makes sense to let those who are wondering know as they contemplate whether becoming a member is right for them. Once the benefits are published, the congregation must authentically deliver on the commitment.

"How Do They Enforce Their Expectations?"

Members of more traditional churches are often somewhat skeptical when they hear stories of these new missional churches. Does Grace Point *really* expect members to give a week of vacation every year to be involved in a stateside mission project, or once every five years to be involved in a global mission partnership? Does Mosaic *really* expect those who become part of the covenant community to assume responsibilities as staff members? Does Fellowship Bible Church *really* expect every adult member to serve on an ongoing basis in a ministry within their community? Then comes the inevitable question: "How do they enforce those expectations?" This question is based on the assumption that most church members are not going to live up to a missional expectation; it reveals the gulf between the two church cultures.

The answer is that real cultural practices do not have to be enforced. In the missional churches we have talked about, the practices described in these accounts are normal and expected. In essence, missional churches are *redefining normal Christianity.* Perhaps the difference with high-threshold membership churches is the difference between acceptance of nominal Christianity and the expectation of normal Christianity. Missional communities are pursuing the kind of faith that was normal in the book of Acts. They believe God is still in the business of using every member of His Body in the accomplishment of His mission.

Another distinction in Alan Roxburgh's missional paradigm is the high level of expectation of members in the covenant community. Those who have covenanted together are perceived as ministers and missionaries of the church. There is little distinction between paid staff members and other members in the community. "Overcoming the professional-shaped leadership models," says Roxburgh, "is an essential shift toward a missional leadership." This issue is perhaps among the most difficult challenges faced by the Western church, which often opts to hire staff members to lead new ministry initiatives toward which the church commits itself.

Mosaic wrestled with this issue of the ambiguity of the term *membership* and made a significant decision regarding the language it uses in referring to those aligning with the church. Pastor Erwin McManus explained the developing process that brought Mosaic to its current language: "For a while we tried the term 'partners.' Starbucks has partners, and we liked that connotation more than some others. But we finally agreed: what we really mean is that when you become a member you come on bi-vocational staff. What you are is a 'tent maker.' For the last several years I stopped calling our staff a staff and started calling them a leadership team."[9]

Today, members are those who have decided to make Mosaic their faith community. Those who have agreed to the Mosaic covenant, formerly called members, are now considered "staff." Those who formerly would have been called staff are now their "leadership team." Former members were "grandfathered"—given a special designation, if they chose not to be considered staff. However, those now coming into the covenant community, making commitment to Mosaic's four areas of member expectations—live evangelistically, minimally tithe, serve in ministry, and live a holy life—come as staff members.

Speaking of the counsel given as individuals come to be part of Mosaic, McManus explained: "We say to them, 'You are on staff. You now have staff responsibility. You have a career and that is your contact for ministry. You have a job. That is your source of income. But you are here on this planet to fulfill the mission of Christ. So you are coming on the staff of Mosaic.'" As a result of this change in language, Mosaic has commissioned more than six hundred staff persons as missionaries to the Los Angeles area. Many who were members before the shift in terminology are taking their roles more seriously. Equally, many who are journeying toward knowing God, but who have not yet come to personal faith, are members of Mosaic. They are part of the learning and serving community.

The Mosaic paradigm is a cutting-edge way of thinking about church membership. Mosaic creates multiple entry points to make it easy for people who have not yet come to faith in Christ to find a place in the fellowship: through celebration (corporate worship experiences), cell groups, and service projects. Anyone who is willing is welcomed to join with Mosaic as the church both ministers and serves people through various ministry initiatives. Mosaic believes that many young adults will first belong (choose to make Mosaic the place where they become part of a fellowship of people who are on the way toward knowing God) and become (begin the process of discipleship) before they grasp the significance of believing (personal salvation by faith in Christ resulting in personal redemption and transformation).

Like all the missional churches I have seen, Mosaic has elevated the expectation of membership to a radical minimum standard that removes nominal Christianity as an option. Members of these churches— ordinary Christians—make world-changing differences every day as they live out Christ's mission.

Reflection and Application

1. Reflect on the current member expectations in your church. What changes can you make that encourage a higher threshold for membership?

2. Compare the occasions for Peter's two calls (Mark 1:17 and John 21:22). What do you think are the implications of the phrase "He has received the grace which costs" (Bonhoeffer, p. 49)?

3. Enlist three members to observe your church's worship experiences as though they were considering membership. Ask them to consider these questions:

- Did I receive clear information on how I could unite with the church?

- Was I informed of opportunities through which I might learn about membership before making that decision?

- Were there options for registering my decisions in which I would be comfortable?

SUGGESTED READING

Bonhoeffer, D. *The Cost of Discipleship*. New York: Macmillan, 1987.
Hanks, B., Jr., and Shell, W. A. (eds.). *Discipleship: Great Insights from the Most Experienced Disciple Makers*. Grand Rapids, Mich.: Zondervan, 1981.

Missional Practice Assessment

Rate each statement that follows from 1 (the statement is not true of our church) to 7 (the statement is true of our church) by circling the appropriate response. The greatest insight will be gained if you avoid selecting 4 as a response. Please use that selection minimally. When you are finished, transfer your responses to the assessments in the Appendix and total your scores to find your net response. Your group's response to these assessments gives a clear picture of your church's readiness to move to being missional.

We have clearly stated expectations of members.

1   2   3   4   5   6   7

We clearly communicate pathways to membership.

1   2   3   4   5   6   7

Members hold one another accountable for fulfilling expectations.

1   2   3   4   5   6   7

We communicate benefits of membership.

1   2   3   4   5   6   7

Significant numbers of pre-Christians identify us as their faith community.

1   2   3   4   5   6   7

We have various entry points through which new members become part of our church.

1   2   3   4   5   6   7

Nominal Christianity is abnormal in our church.

1   2   3   4   5   6   7

4

MISSIONAL PRACTICE NUMBER TWO

BE REAL, NOT REAL RELIGIOUS

Many tax-gatherers and sinners were dining with
Jesus and his disciples; for there were many
of them and they were following Him.

—Mark 2:15

Here is one who comfortably sits in the midst of those outside
religious circles. Jesus is not threatened by their irreligious
lifestyles nor does he intimidate them by His divinity. He chooses
to introduce His incarnate presence into secular surroundings.

—Bill Tinsley, *Authentic Disciple*

TWENTY YEARS AGO, Southlake, Texas, was just a "wide place in the road." But it was less than ten miles from the location destined to become Dallas–Fort Worth International Airport, and property values began to escalate as people sought to locate near the international hub. Southlake's population soon doubled, and then doubled again. Suddenly, thousands of people lived there. The town's infrastructure was woefully outpaced by exponential growth. With the rapid influx of developers, the city set stringent guidelines for commercial building permits. Although Southlake had never had a "downtown" or central business district, among the first commercial centers approved for construction was a development in which buildings were made to look as though they were constructed in a bygone era. Where none had ever existed, Southlake built an old downtown with shops designed around greenways and parks!

From a distance, downtown Southlake looks authentic. Newcomers might think they stumbled on old downtown Southlake. But they soon discover that even though it is a beautiful piece of urban architecture, the center is really no different from the ubiquitous malls that otherwise dot the landscape. Same stores. Same retail chains. Same products. Only the outside is different.

In 1994, I attended a continuing education event at Overseas Ministries Study Center across the street from Yale University in New Haven, Connecticut. Without a car for days, I enjoyed walks to a neighborhood near the campus that was home to a diverse collection of businesses and restaurants in buildings that had been there for many decades. Mornings I could enjoy a fresh-baked bagel and coffee and conversation with the owner-operator of a small bakery. Lunch might be a slice of New York style pizza, eaten at one of two sidewalk tables of a small establishment. The Chinese grocery also served made-to-order prepared food. There I enjoyed meals at tables arranged in a narrow room adjacent to the grocery. There were dry cleaners, furniture stores, and other retail businesses. There were no chain stores in the neighborhood. In stark contrast to Southlake Center, trash receptacles were sometimes in view, much of the décor was well worn, and not every odor was commercially altered for palatability.

Southlake looked authentic. New Haven *was* authentic. Can you guess which experience I preferred?

Authenticity does not reproduce well. Creating an old downtown aesthetic filled with traditional "mall stores" does not create an authentic experience. Authenticity is not only about appearance. It is the sounds, smells, products, and wastes resulting from the creation and consumption of the diverse staples of a particular culture.

The hunger for authenticity is epidemic today. This hunger extends beyond goods and services to relationships, ideas, and spirituality. Can such faith can be found within the traditional church? John Drane doesn't think so. In *The McDonaldization of the Church*, he writes, "People are unlikely to be attracted to the church which, as they see it, has become a place with too much religion and too little spirituality. . . . One of the ways [spirituality] will be contrasted with 'religion' will be as an all-embracing reality that can give meaning to the whole of life."[1]

Churches, once among the most respected community institutions, have lost status as places of significant impact. Where their voice once possessed authority, their words now fall on deaf ears. Alex Kotlowitz's Pulitzer Prize–winning account of the lives of two brothers being raised in the Henry Horner Housing Project in Chicago portrayed the experience of many concerning the church:

> For a few months last spring, [Pharaoh, the younger brother, had] attended Bible classes at the First Congregational Baptist Church. Washington Boulevard was lined with churches, but most of them now served people who had since moved from the neighborhood. *Churches had lost their authority in areas like Horner.* Pharaoh grew bored with the classes and began to question whether there was indeed a God. He often prayed to him, asking that he let them move from the projects, but Pharaoh would say, "I be praying but he don't do nothing. Maybe there ain't no God." It was as much a question as it was a statement.[2]

Loss of authority results when there is no congruence between words and actions, between presentation and practices. Authority is lost when something only looks like the real thing. If we attend church but don't find God, where are we? Missional churches are seeking to reclaim a place of authority by proving the reality of their message through their lives. They are seeking to be real, but not real religious.

Fellowship Bible Church in Little Rock wrestled with the issue of authenticity as they began to reshape themselves into a church more accurately reflecting God's missional heart. The church had experienced growth, but pastor Robert Lewis sensed the church was not building bridges into their community. Through soul searching, they sought answers to difficult questions concerning the authenticity of their presence in the area. Out of this painful introspection, Lewis remarked, "To our age, truth is nothing more than talk. . . . Our postmodern world is tired of words—it wants *real*."[3]

Missional churches express "real" in a number of ways:

- They show authenticity in faith.
- They are authentic with one another.
- They act authentically in the world.

They Show Authenticity in Faith

Spirituality is much more than religious practices. Many voices decry established religions as out-of-touch with the real state of the human condition. They perceive the church to be a head trip that never touches the heart. How unlike the Christianity portrayed in scripture is that assessment! There, faith emoted from the deepest parts of the human being. The Christian faith does not address only the head; it touches the depth of emotions, the senses, and the inner person. Contemporary versions have translated the New Testament word *splanchna* with various terms such as heart or inward parts. Those familiar with the King James text might recall the phrase "bowels of compassion," used to denote the inner depth touched by Christian love. Authentic faith is not empty words; it is an experiential reality.

Missional churches are communities of authentic disciples. These churches take discipleship seriously. The degree to which they hold one another accountable touches every part of their lives and has implications every day of the week. Missional faith is not a Sunday religion, but a vibrant relationship with the God of mission. This is why missional churches are so attractive to spiritual seekers. The genuineness of their faith experience is appealing to those who hunger for something more than organized religion.

Missional churches are captivated by the mystery of faith, the wonder of being in God's presence, and the joy of serving in His Kingdom. Their God is real, and their faith is real. Not a bunch of religious rules to follow, this faith relates people with their Creator through His Son. As Joseph Stowell wrote: "A set of rules is rarely worth denying our passions their pleasure; valued relationships are always worth self-denial. This is what set authentic Christianity apart from other religious systems and philosophies. Christianity is first and foremost a relationship—a relationship with Christ as the defining and motivating reality of followership."[4] More than a system of religious rules, missional discipleship is a life-changing relationship, a Body in love with God.

They Are Authentic with One Another

Spirituality and faith are expressed in relationship with others in community. The testimony of first-century Christians was enhanced by unselfish love as they made room in their hearts for one another (Acts 2:32–37). In fact, as a displaced community of pilgrim people, citizens of another Kingdom, their actions in community reflected a different culture. Missional Christianity is a counterculture movement.

In this movement, communities are established across racial and socioeconomic lines, replacing division with unity. Countering culture's hostility, missional communities express hospitality. Where skepticism creates doubt, missional communities grant trust. Instead of isolated loneliness, Christian community draws people together as friends. Loneliness and fear are expunged by the combined faith, hope, and love of those persons who covenant together as a community on mission with God. Each individual's awareness of how far he or she is from being shaped by God's heart results in grateful acknowledgment of the missional community as a place for becoming. Together they are a community under construction, being refashioned into His likeness by His Spirit (2 Corinthians 3:18).

In a society that expects instant everything, missional communities know their mutual pursuit, being shaped by God's heart, is a process that takes time. Those who make up missional communities give space for others in the community to make mistakes as they mature as disciples of Jesus Christ. In *Dangerous Wonder,* Michael Yaconelli reminds us that mistakes are expected: "Mistakes are the guaranteed consequence of wild abandon. Mistakes are signs of growth. That is why the Old and New Testament are full of people who made mistakes. The church should be the one place in our culture where mistakes are not only expected but welcomed."[5]

Mistakes can be in areas where ambiguity exists, pursuit of a vision is subsequently proven wrong, or there is rebellion against clear directives of Scripture. Some churches simply ignore the mistakes of those within the fellowship, choosing not to confront. Missional churches believe authentic relationships create responsibilities among those in community. Those responsibilities include confronting, forgiving, and restoring one another. Where these responsibilities are enacted, believers experience confession and grace, learn from their mistakes, and thus are empowered to face similar circumstances in the future.

Jamye Miller of Christ Fellowship has seen his fellowship lovingly confront sin in the lives of fellow believers. Confrontation is done privately, personally, and honestly. In his experience, the only way a church becomes "real" enough to "speak the truth in love" is through establishing authentic relationships that value personal accountability. Christ Fellowship knows the purity of the Body is directly proportional to the honesty and accountability among members. At Christ Fellowship, intimacy develops in Lifegroups, small cells in which members relate as an authentic Christian community.

Similarly, Neil Cole, executive director of Church Multiplication Associates and an experienced church planter and pastor, advocates for Life Transformation Groups (LTG), a structure employed by various missional communities. A Life Transformation Group is intentionally small, intended to be no more than three people (when a fourth person comes to be part, two groups of two begin). The LTG is designed for disciple growth and accountability. It consists of three essential disciplines for personal spiritual growth: a steady diet of Scripture, confession of sin, and prayer for others who need Christ. In the LTG, participants discuss insights from the twenty-five to thirty chapters of Scripture they read every week, hold one another accountable through responding to a series of questions in a vulnerable and honest environment, and spend time praying for friends who do not yet have a relationship with Christ.[6]

Without regard to the designation used, missional churches involve members in relationship with other believers through small groups or cells. It is in this environment that community life is most deeply influenced. There, members experience the intimacy of Body life that practices the extensive *one another* commands of the New Testament.

At Antioch Community Church, Lifegroups are the church's primary support system. It is through these cells that members encourage one another toward maturity and service as disciples. Lifegroup leaders encourage groups to interact with one another in seven areas that are based upon the New Testament:

1. Love one another (John 13:34–35; John 15:12, 17; 1 Thessalonians 3:12; 1 Thessalonians 4:9; Hebrews 10:24; 1 Peter 1:22; 1 John 3:11, 23; 1 John 4:7, 11, 12)

2. Yield to others, serving their interests: be devoted (Romans 12:10); humility (1 Peter 5:5), submit (Hebrews 13:13, Ephesians 5:21; 1 Peter 5:5); serve (Galatians 5:13; Hebrews 10:24)

3. Spend time with one another: greet (Romans 16:16; 1 Corinthians 16:20; 2 Corinthians 13:12; 1 Peter 5:14); hospitality (1 Peter 4:9); have fellowship (1 John 1:7)

4. Allow others to be imperfect—don't become irritated with them: be patient (Ephesians 4:2; Colossians 3:13); accept (Romans 15:7); bear with (Galatians 6:2; Colossians 3:13); be at peace (Mark 9:50); wait for (1 Corinthians 11:33); forgive (Ephesians 4:32)

5. Build one another up with words—be helpful to one another: build up (Romans 14:19; 1 Thessalonians 5:11; Hebrews 3:13); speak truth (Ephesians 4:25; Colossians 3:9); admonish (Romans 15:14;

Colossians 3:16; Hebrews 10:24–25); confess (James 5:16); pray (James 5:16)

6. Have a gentle heart toward others in difficulty: care for (1 Corinthians 12:25); comfort (1 Thessalonians 4:18); be kind (Ephesians 4:32); have compassion (1 Peter 3:8)

7. Be in unity with one another: same mind (Romans 12:16; Ephesians 4:25); members (Romans 12:5; Romans 15:5)[7]

Active observance of these seven areas of relationship results in a culture quite distinct from the world. It is this kind of community that potential members and spiritual searchers enter as they visit Antioch Community Church. One understands why people find the church warm and caring.

They Act Authentically in the World

It is not enough to be nice to one another inside the church. Missional churches treat one another in ways that reflect how they also engage the world. As indicated, they love God and live His mission. In His incarnation He came not to be served, but to serve. Therefore, His missional church does the same. It occupies the role of servant to society. Through ministry, the Word is again being fleshed out.

This is the living proof that Fellowship Bible Church determined to give people outside their congregation. Lewis's description of church is "a community of people who stand firm in the truth over time against raging currents of opposition and who present living proof of a loving God to a watching world."[8] It is reflected not only through the church's organized ministries into the community; in fact, its authenticity is most vividly seen when the church is not together in ministry.

The litmus test of the missional church is how members live when scattered during the week. They must prove the validity of their transforming faith in schools, sports teams, at the office, and on the golf course. When their faith transforms the way they live and react everyday, then it merits the world's attention. Marion Wade's life goal was to serve other people and run a business through which he could live his values daily, not just on weekends. As founder of ServiceMaster, he instilled principles of faith into his company. The sixth of their twenty-one leadership principles is "If you don't live it, you don't believe it."[9] Missional churches are instilling the same commitment to authenticity in their members. For them, faith is not something to be held, but something to be lived.

NorthWood Church for the Communities begins to instill the importance of members' authenticity in the everyday world during new-member orientation. In an impassioned emphasis upon personal holiness, with a prophetic tenor, new members encounter these words in NorthWood's *Pilgrim's Progress Guide:*

> The true church is the bride of Christ, and for it to be real, we must be pure. There is a process and period of testing that must be endured to be prepared to stand before him. The bride will be there—the only question is—how clean, how white, how holy will she be?
>
> The credibility of the church today is under incredible fire because she is not real. She is not holy, she has no message different from the rest of the world. She lifts her standards up and makes her claims, imposes them on others and yet does not live them herself.
>
> The whole point of the Sermon on the Mount was to show us what real living is all about. Authenticity means real and genuine. Not fake, no imitation, no hype—reality.[10]

One certainly cannot say NorthWood is going soft! They understand that unless church members live consistent faith in the world, there is no hope that her corporate message will be accepted as authentic. As members live consistently and serve passionately in their everyday spheres of influence, the church becomes the church of irresistible influence.

Being Real in Two Worlds

Back in 1962, when *The Beverly Hillbillies* first aired, most American audiences couldn't stop laughing at the antics of a poor hillbilly family transported to a life of luxury in Beverly Hills. What made that program so funny? Ultimately, the humor of *The Beverly Hillbillies* centered around a clash of cultures. A possum lumbering across a highway might look like "dinner on the hoof" to a native of the back hills, but among the elite of Beverly Hills, the animal was simply a driving annoyance and potential cause for a call to Animal Control. Neither was right or wrong. But it was funny when Granny caught the possum and invited proper guests to dinner!

The Christian church is of a Kingdom culture, but she lives in the world's culture. She does so at the pleasure of Christ, who prayed this for His followers: "I do not ask You to take them out of the world, but to keep them from the evil one. They are not of the world, even as I am not of the world" (John 17:15–16). These words precede his purpose-filled observation, "As You did send Me into the world, I have also sent them into the world."

The church is sent into the world, citizens of one Kingdom, living in another. But our presence should not result in the world's laughter at our inability to relate. We are not Beverly Hillbillies. The colloquial judgment "They were so heavenly minded, they were of no earthly good!" should *not* be applied to the church. The missional church is sent by Christ in the continuance of His mission. He was also from another culture. The incarnation is the story of His relocation for the singular purpose of redemption. Although He came from the presence of the Father, His personality resulted in invitations to the homes of tax gatherers and sinners. They did not always understand Him. They certainly did not all surrender to His ultimate Lordship. But neither was His demeanor such that they sought to avoid Him. He modeled being real, but not real religious. In fact, it was the latter that resulted in His being accused by religious leaders. He castigated those who promoted accretions of religious tradition that prevented people from entering into relationship with God. He was heavenly minded. He was real.

Today the missional church is taking lessons from the Master. It seeks to be real, but not real religious. Real in spirituality. Real in relationships. Jim Herrington, executive director of Mission Houston, issues this challenge: "Without authentic spiritual and relational vitality in a local gathering of believers, the church does not have the resources that are demanded to engage transformation and to influence the world. As the pace of change accelerates, the demand for this power is only going to increase."[11]

May *real* power multiply!

Reflection and Application

1. On the basis of what you have read and understood in this chapter, identify five means through which your congregation will begin to encourage (or already does encourage) authenticity within the Body.

2. Get a pack of four-by-six-inch cards. On each one, write a "one another" command from the Bible. Include:

Confess your sins to one another (James 5:16)

Do not grumble against one another (James 5:9)

Live in harmony with one another (Romans 12:16)

Don't be puffed up against one another (1 Corinthians 4:6)

Admonish one another (Colossians 3:16)

Pray for one another (James 5:16)

Love one another (John 13:34)

Fellowship with one another (1 John 1:7)

Accept one another (Romans 15:7)

Depend on one another (Romans 12:5)

Now gather a group of church members, and randomly give one card to each person. Ask the first person to read the "one another" command and place it on a table or floor. Then ask a second person to read, and place the card either above or below the previous person's card depending upon which command they perceive the church obeys more readily. Continue until all cards have been "played."

Encourage dialogue to develop around the commands as they are "played." Note which commands are near the bottom of the stack of cards, ask if those commands are less important, and discuss why they are less readily observed. Allow members to define authenticity in light of what they observed in the exercise.

Suggested Reading

Arterburn, S., and Luck, K. *Everyman, God's Man: Every Man's Guide to Courageous Faith and Daily Integrity.* Colorado Springs: Waterbrook Press, 2003.

Bonhoeffer, D. *Life Together: A Discussion of Christian Fellowship.* San Francisco: HarperCollins, 1954.

Martin, G., and McIntosh, G. *Creating Community: Deeper Fellowship Through Small Group Ministry.* Nashville: Broadman and Holman, 1997.

McMinn, D. *The 11th Commandment: Experiencing the One Anothers of Scripture.* Irving, Tex.: 6Acts Press, 2000.

Missional Practice Assessment

Rate each statement that follows from 1 (the statement is not true of our church) to 7 (the statement is true of our church) by circling the appropriate response. The greatest insight will be gained if you avoid selecting 4 as a response. Please use that selection minimally. When you are finished, transfer your responses to the assessments in the Appendix and total your scores to find your net response. Your group's response to these assessments gives a clear picture of your church's readiness to move to being missional.

Our message is validated by our actions in the community.

1   2   3   4   5   6   7

Members do not "wear masks" with one another.

1   2   3   4   5   6   7

People in the community see our church as vital.

1   2   3   4   5   6   7

Members trust one another enough to confess their sin.

1   2   3   4   5   6   7

Members are incorporated into small groups for growth
and accountability.

1   2   3   4   5   6   7

We prioritize member involvement with unchurched people.

1   2   3   4   5   6   7

Our culture makes it easy for people to admit unanswered
questions about their faith.

1   2   3   4   5   6   7

MISSIONAL PRACTICE NUMBER THREE

TEACH TO OBEY RATHER THAN TO KNOW

But He said, "On the contrary, blessed are those who hear the word of God and observe it."

—Luke 11:28

We must be aware of resting in the mere letter [of scripture] without expecting through the indwelling Holy Spirit a real and living experience of all that the Scripture holds out to our faith.

—William Law, *The Power of the Spirit*

NO ONE CAN BE PART of the church without possessing faith. Many churches, however, do not equip members to express the faith they possess. So members continue to be reminded what a Christian *is,* without gaining clear biblical counsel regarding what a Christian *does.* Faith possessed must become faith expressed if God's purpose for each believer is to be realized.

Faith can be known. But unless it is observed, can it be real? Activist preacher Jim Wallis says, "In the Bible, faith is not something you possess but rather something you practice. You have to put it into action or it

really doesn't mean anything. Faith changes things. It's the energy of transformation, both for individuals and for a society."[1]

Religious systems have long specialized in the transfer of spiritual
knowledge, but they have an equally long heritage of producing enlight-
ened followers whose lifestyles remain unchanged by that spiritual knowledge. "Even so, faith, if it has no works, is dead, being by itself. But
someone may well say, 'You have faith, and I have works: show me your
faith without the works, and I will show you my faith by my works'"
(James 2:17–18).

Jesus' admonition to the scribes and Pharisees confirms this reality:
"Woe to you, scribes and Pharisees, hypocrites! For you tithe mint and
dill and cumin, and have neglected the weightier provisions of the law:
justice and mercy and faithfulness. . . . Even so you too outwardly appear
righteous to men, but inwardly you are full of hypocrisy and lawlessness"
(Matthew 23:23, 28).

Missional churches are not satisfied simply to transfer biblical knowledge. Their goal is members' obedience to spiritual revelation. It is not
what they know, but what they live that counts. Missional churches teach
to obey rather than simply to know. To accomplish this:

- They equip believers.
- They practice "applied Christianity."
- They have a high commitment to God's Word.
- They learn obedience through disciplines.
- They use a variety of methods.

They Equip Believers

When I asked Grace Point's Jeff Harris to describe the Christian education processes designed and used to equip believers, he responded:

> What we do is "high-octane" training with the DNA of who we are
> in everything we do. Equipping is done in "existing time slots" (times
> when members are already committed to participating in church activ-
> ities). Every new member participates in "Discovery" with other new
> members. This class provides a clear introduction to our basic beliefs,
> helps new members learn their S.H.A.P.E. for Ministry (a combination
> of spiritual gifts, heart, abilities, personality, and experience), and con-
> nects them with a Point Person, a 360 Community (for Bible study and
> fellowship) and a servant group.

> Servant groups are where members learn to live out their gifts. All servant groups cover our core values repeatedly. Every six weeks we hold "Summit" in which all servant groups come together to celebrate our core values with teaching and application of those values portrayed. It is a dynamic process contextualized for all ages using the best materials available. We are not locked in to a particular "curriculum" but use what we believe to be the best in any given area of growth.[2]

Did you notice that he tucked Bible study away in the middle of his response to a question about their Christian education process? It was deeply embedded between preliminary new-member orientation (personal self-awareness of God's shaping through passion, spiritual gifting, and environmental issues) and members' expression of service in ministry. By the very nature of that embedding, Bible study is not an end unto itself but rather prepares members for living out their faith. It gives guidance to the rest of the laboratory experience that is the total Christian education process of Grace Point.

In response to the same question, Bob Roberts, pastor of NorthWood Church for the Communities, offered insight regarding the new role of equipping in a postmodern era. "Curriculum is a modern form of training for the most part today," he told me:

> It makes religion more cognitive. While we do use some of the best materials we can find, we believe that equipping for discipleship requires believers to have a daily worship time. They must be living with interactive relationships where faith is being discussed and fashioned. We believe for people to be transformed they must get alone with God. We teach them to journal while they are reading His word. That way they are hearing His voice, noting questions about implications and meanings of what they have heard. They are prepared to discuss those things with others in the community.[3]

Harris embedded traditional "Christian education" into the larger context of preparing members to live their faith; Roberts directly acknowledged his concern that education be more than a cognitive experience. Some might use the term *cognitive faith* as a descriptor of what has historically been called theology. *Theology* is "a word about God." It is the study of God. One can pass academic courses in theology by knowing answers to questions about the person and attributes of God. No relationship with Him is required. Theology can be limited to cognitive information. One can read and study the Bible theologically, for what it teaches about God.

Mosaic's Erwin McManus affirmed equipping as more than the transfer of biblical knowledge. Concerning Christian education or equipping, he said, "I think that in the traditional church what you oftentimes have is the affirmation of beliefs, and that's how people get fed. In a missional church it's the implementation of the actions of beliefs and the fleshing out of beliefs. We actually hold ourselves more fundamentally to the scripture. Honestly, I think most traditional churches don't really *obey* the scriptures."[4] Earlier, he discussed a missional hermeneutic: "God never intended the Bible to be studied for information or knowledge alone. . . . It is significant that the history of the first-century church is called the book of Acts, not the book of Truths."[5]

The goal of biblical instruction in the missional church is obedience, not simply knowledge. Because of what has been studied, the life ethic of members should be altered. As Matt Hannan of New Heights explains it, "Discipleship is not what you know; discipleship is what you do. Therefore, disciple training can't be in knowing; disciple training has to be in doing." Successful equipping involves movement from information through contemplation to transformation.

Years after graduating from seminary, church planter Ron Nolen remembers "three objectives of teaching" he learned as a student from professor Jack Terry: knowledge gain, attitude change, and conduct response. Unfortunately, Nolen observes, most churches design their equipping ministries only for the first of those objectives. Authentic discipleship requires getting to the third response. For missional churches, discipleship includes information that changes attitudes and alters conduct.

They Practice "Applied Christianity"

Glenda Hope ministers to the poor, homeless, and drug-addicted residents of San Francisco's Tenderloin District. Serving since 1972 as executive director of San Francisco Network Ministries, Hope advocates new paradigms for theological education, including training done in the contexts of ministry rather than in sterile classrooms. She applies a multitier structure to Christian education that she attributes to W. J. Bousma.

In an address at San Francisco Theological Seminary, Bousma stated, "Spirituality bears to theology somewhat the relation of practice to theory or of action to contemplation. . . . Spirituality is first-order Christianity; theology is second-order Christianity."[6] According to Hope, theology is the primary arena of academicians and theological educators, while spirituality is the primary arena of practitioners of ministry. In summary, Hope quotes Bousma: "For those who are in daily touch with suffering, needy, sinful humanity, what is *most* required is less theology than spirituality, *applied* Christianity, first-order Christianity."

Perhaps this paradigm can serve to assist missional churches as they seek to articulate their equipping ministries. Neither Bousma nor Hope denies the significance of reflective thinking regarding biblical information—theology. What they advocate is the application of Christian teachings through life-transforming relevance—applied Christianity. In a society hungering for spiritual experience but questioning religious structures, first-order Christianity is a refreshing wind of God's Spirit, welcomed for its relevant authenticity in the personal context.

The missional church seeks to teach members to obey rather than simply to know. It does not however, lessen the validity of theological reflection. What is *known* of God is enhanced by *obedience,* as disciples observe the impact of His Word in the everyday lives of people on the journey toward being shaped by God's heart.

They Have a High Commitment to God's Word

Teaching to obey underscores the high commitment to God's Word found in missional communities. Whether in corporate worship, personal devotion, equipping ministries, cells, or Life Transformation Groups, these congregations respect the Bible and its capacity to impart life direction for disciples of Jesus Christ.

Communities often have doctrinal statements succinctly summarizing the essence of their beliefs, but it is their practices that most effectively demonstrate the same. Doctrinal statements include communities' understanding of the Bible. For instance, the Antioch Community states: "We believe the Bible is the inspired, authoritative, living, eternally reliable Word of God equally in all parts and without error in its original manuscript, absolutely infallible, and our source of supreme revelation from God, superior to conscience and reason, though not contrary to reason; and it is therefore our infallible rule of faith and practice and necessary to our daily lives (2 Timothy 3:16–17; 1 Peter 1:23–25; Hebrews 4:12)."

In listing "The Essentials We Believe," NorthWood Church for the Communities includes this essential belief: "The Bible is God's Word to us. It was written by human authors, under the supernatural guidance of the Holy Spirit. It is the supreme source of truth for Christian beliefs and living. Because it is inspired by God, it is the truth without any mixture of error (2 Timothy 3:16; 2 Peter 1:20–21; 2 Timothy 1:13; Psalm 119:105, 160; Psalm 12:6; Proverbs 30:5)."

NorthWood transfers beliefs into practices; following the statement concerning the Bible, the practical implication is stated: "Since God's Word is the only completely reliable and truthful authority, we accept the Bible as our manual for living. Our first question when faced with a decision is 'What does the Bible say?' We practice daily Bible reading, Bible study and Bible memorization. The Bible is the basis for all we believe."

Similar statements can be found in materials designed to communicate beliefs of other missional communities. One of Mosaic's "five core convictions" states: "The Bible is God's authoritative word to us." However, high commitment to God's Word is not only indicated through formal statements, it is also evidenced in classes offered, in cell group study emphases, and other tacit examples.

At New Heights Church, the Scripture text for the sermon (in their dechurched language, "Today's Talk") is reproduced and handed to all attending. Printed from a contemporary translation, the bottom of the page encourages: "If you don't own a modern translation of the Bible, please visit our Information Center to receive a complimentary New Testament." Although very simple, things that virtually any church could do, the printed text and offer of a free modern translation New Testament affirm the value New Heights places upon Scripture.

They Learn Obedience Through Disciplines

Missional communities help members obey scripture through emphasis placed on classical Christian disciplines. Two extremes must be avoided as communities seek to give opportunity for growth in personal spirituality. On the one hand, some individuals understand practices to be "laws" to which Christians must adhere if they are to grow as disciples. This legalistic scripting of the Christian experience leads to moral bankruptcy through dependence upon personal works. On the other extreme are those who indicate practices have no import in developing authentic discipleship. These tend toward the extreme of antinomianism, suggesting because disciples are born as a result of God's grace and not of their own works there is no purpose in observing any "practices" as disciples. Both extremes can be destructive to the development of authentic disciples.

Though they understand the disciplines hold no special power or grace, missional communities are leading believers to initiate practices that place them, before God and within the community, in positions where righteousness and holy lifestyle may be developed. Classically, the disciplines have been identified as inward, outward, and corporate. Quaker author and minister Richard Foster has had much influence in leading missional communities to reclaim the practice of the disciplines. His insights have led many evangelical Christians to reconnect with personal spirituality, widely experienced in previous generations but virtually lost in the technologically driven culture of the West. In his writing, Foster investigates the classic spiritual disciplines identified in three arenas: inward (Bible study, meditation, prayer, and fasting), outward (solitude, submission, service, and simplicity), and corporate (worship, confession, celebration, and guidance).[7]

Missional communities are building those disciplines into the lives of believers in various ways. We have already alluded to cells and other small groups built around disciplines of Bible study and prayer. Accountability within these groups also serves to offer mutual guidance.

Service is being expressed as members participate in ministries. At Mosaic, McManus has found the most significant means to ensure that those who are new to the church remain is to involve them immediately in serving. He observes: "For us, mobilization equals assimilation. If we get them involved, they will be here. The number one factor is, 'Are they serving?' If they are, they will still be here a year from now. If not, they will likely be gone." Interestingly, Mosaic's servant ministries have been the portals not only through which many have become active in the Mosaic community but through which individuals have come to personal faith in Christ. Invited to serve before they understood what it meant to become a Christian, serving alongside those who knew Christ authenticated the message they heard proclaimed by Mosaic.

The discipline of simplicity is of paramount importance in a consumer-driven society. In my conversation with Darrell Guder, he expressed this concern: "I think about all the families in our churches who go home on Sundays and spend the rest of the week trying to figure out how they are going to get out of the burden of indebtedness they are in," he said. "How are they going to overthrow the idol of credit cards and credit indebtedness? What church is talking about the captivity to wealth that people are literally struggling with in their homes? These are all forms of equipping. We can do Bible study in our churches and not be touching a single issue that really affects how that missionary vocation happens outside the church."[8]

Missional communities such as Christ Fellowship and New Heights Church are finding specific ways to equip members in the discipline of simplicity. To speak practically to the issue of simplicity, Jamye Miller felt led to give away the furniture in his family's home, opting for the simplest accoutrements. Miller's family now enjoys "being able to kick the beach ball with the children in the house without having to worry about breaking things." Upon seeing the sparse furnishings, people visiting their home will often ask, "Oh, have you guys just moved in?" It was painful for the moment, but the family now enjoys freedom from so many "things that must be cared for." For members of New Heights, principles of simplicity are routinely taught in a popular course called "Your Money Matters." Described as a financial management seminar, promotional materials state: "Managing your money well can make a big difference for you, for your family, and others. This seminar will take you through the most important areas of financial management, and those areas where most of us make common mistakes."

They Use a Variety of Methods

Perhaps the most traditional method of instruction in the Western church is the Sunday School or Church School. Whether offered primarily for children or designed for all ages, this structure was among the most widely used for Bible teaching in churches during the twentieth century. Among the strengths of the structure was the age-graded organization, ensuring a designated place for anyone who attended. The school has been effectively used to reach and involve new members in Bible study and fellowship. Classes were places where members expressed concern for each other, experienced fellowship, and followed a systematic plan for Bible study. Frequently using educational curricula designed specifically for this structure, members were encouraged to "study their lesson" before coming to the weekly class.

Although the structure has organizational strengths, it has generally not been recognized as having transformational impact upon the lives of most students. William A. Beckham, who has done extensive research on the function and use of small groups in churches, says that Sunday school is set up as an informational system rather than a transformational system. He further states, "We can become spiritually dry even with orthodox theology, a love of God's Word, faithfulness to the church and a personal devotional life."[9] He contends the church must include both large and small groups, addressing the head and the heart, intellect and experience within the context of accountability.

Some communities continue to furnish the Sunday school structure while also offering cell groups, Lifegroups, or other structures designed for a higher level of accountability in personal holiness and spiritual growth. In addition to small-group structures, missional communities have reclaimed the value of one-to-one relationships for growth, accountability, and encouragement. Mentoring has long been an apprenticeship model for instruction. Placing a learner with a master in an environment where a particular skill or activity can be learned has high yield. Waylon Moore has invested his life in mentoring church leaders. His passion for mentoring is derived from Christ's method: "Jesus said, 'Follow me,' not, 'Listen to me.' We learn by doing. Words are a poor substitute for a picture. . . . If you want to encourage [a] man to study the Bible daily, invite him to meet with you to see how you are doing it. . . . Otherwise, he will become tragically dependent upon others for being fed from the Scriptures."[10]

Few students ever learn to play piano in a classroom setting. They study individually with a teacher. Medical students may invest many hours in classrooms and laboratories, but their ultimate learning experiences occur in residency programs where they observe and practice medicine under the auspices of qualified physicians. Jenny Myer is employed by Harley-Davidson and is responsible for "Rider's Edge," the company's twenty-five-hour course teaching uninitiated Harley-Davidson customers basic riding skills. The success of the course is built upon one primary philosophy: "We don't just explain, we let them experience." During the course, participants go from being pushed on a bike to riding solo with confidence. It was also experience that resulted in the growth of John, Mark, and Timothy, or Aquilla and Priscilla in the New Testament. Their development was enhanced most by accompanying Paul and Barnabas in mission experiences, not just hearing them explain God's mission.

Members of Grace Point Church view their mentoring process as a primary method of spiritual development. All members participate in "360 Relationships," which include a Barnabas (mentor), Silas (peer), and Timothy (disciple). Grace Point's description of each part of this relationship is revealing:[11]

YOU AND YOUR MENTOR (BARNABAS)

Your mentor is a person you respect, is accessible and with whom you have a relationship. A mentor possesses wisdom, knowledge, experience and spiritual maturity beyond your own. Your mentor should also be responsive, that is you can expect answers or be given the means to find the answers you seek within a reasonable time frame.

YOU AND YOUR PEER (SILAS)

Perhaps our most understandable description of this person is an accountability relationship. An effective accountability relationship should provide for mutual disclosure and access. That is, there are no secrets and either one can inspect the life of the other at any time. Mutual honesty means that the relationship must be based on truth telling and not approval seeking. For that to happen, an accountability partner must be someone you trust. Since more than 85 percent of communication is nonverbal, regular face-to face interaction with your accountability partner is necessary. With the goal of developing a relationship of full devotion to Jesus Christ, an effective and meaningful accountability relationship should include a mutual desire for transformation in the areas disclosed. From time to time, accountability relationships will find it helpful to do an assessment of the progress they are making. Finally, there should be an element of modeling with each person seeking the leadership of the Holy Spirit to live the Christian life. We are seeking to be imitators of Christ and in so doing become models for one another.

YOU AND YOUR DISCIPLE (TIMOTHY)
This is the relationship in which you invest yourself in the life of another for the purpose of their spiritual development. You take on the responsibility for modeling the Christian life. The discipler and the disciple must spend intentional time together, assess what the disciple's needs are and then develop a plan with the appropriate tools, such as a Christian Life Profile, to address those needs. The disciple should be prepared to complete assignments given by the discipler and be willing to be held accountable for their completion. The ultimate goal of this relationship is multiplication. That is, the disciple in whom the character of Christ is being developed would, in turn, undertake the discipling of another.

Not every missional community has developed its mentoring processes to this extent. Some would not prefer the degree of structure found therein. But missional churches are committed to equipping authentic disciples of Jesus Christ, and that commitment cannot be fulfilled in the absence of one-to-one learning. The equipping structures of missional churches must be multifaceted, incorporating various learning techniques, accommodating visual, auditory, and tactile learners for their own missional task as disciples.

Charles Van Engen, originator of the term *missional,* writes from his academic perspective as a trainer of church leaders. He calls for the reduction of any knowledge gulf between "clergy" and "laity." His vision of theological education would find its most significant expression in the lives of everyday Christians living as authentic disciples in the accomplishment of God's mission: "Our educational programs in the Church must be understood to be the equipping of the people of God for a dynamically missional discipleship in service to the world. . . . It no longer will be the pursuit of some mysterious academic discipline open only to a few initiates. Rather, theological education must teach the essentials of biblical faith in order to mobilize all the people of God to live out in day-to-day existence the implications of their radical discipleship."[12]

Missional communities echo the professor's desire. Their goal is to teach disciples to obey rather than simply to know. They are committed to invest in the lives of church members until the words of Friedrich Nietzsche can be applied to them: "The essential thing 'in heaven and earth' is . . . that there should be long obedience in the same direction; there thereby results, and has always resulted in the long run, something which has made life worth living."[13]

Reflection and Application

1. Discuss the implications of the phrase "We will not teach beyond obedience." Predict potential changes in your church's Bible study groups were these implications to be followed. How might classes be modified to emphasize application in addition to knowledge?

2. Explain these two statements in light of missional practice number three: teach to obey rather than simply to know:

- Teaching requires the transmission of ideas and concepts.
- Equipping requires the transmission of learned skills.[14]

3. What is required for us to be able to interpret the Bible? Write a paragraph comparing the authority of Scripture and the disciple's competence in Christ.

SUGGESTED READING

Clinton, R. J. *The Making of a Leader.* Colorado Springs: Navpress, 1988.
Warren, R. *Twelve Dynamic Bible Study Methods.* Wheaton, Ill.: Victor Books, 1981.

Missional Practice Assessment

Rate each statement that follows from 1 (the statement is not true of our church) to 7 (the statement is true of our church) by circling the appropriate response. The greatest insight will be gained if you avoid selecting 4 as a response. Please use that selection minimally. When you are finished, transfer your responses to the assessments in the Appendix and total your scores to find your net response. Your group's response to these assessments gives a clear picture of your church's readiness to move to being missional.

We have a high regard for the Word of God.

1   2   3   4   5   6   7

Members are equipped to practice spiritual disciplines.

1   2   3   4   5   6   7

Our teaching ministries emphasize moving from knowledge to obedience.

1   2   3   4   5   6   7

We partner new believers with existing members in learning relationships.

1   2   3   4   5   6   7

We challenge members to be responsible in their obedience to God.

1   2   3   4   5   6   7

We excel in equipping members to apply Bible knowledge to real-life situations.

1   2   3   4   5   6   7

We hold one another accountable for obeying God's Word.

1   2   3   4   5   6   7

6

MISSIONAL PRACTICE NUMBER FOUR

REWRITE WORSHIP EVERY WEEK

---

*All the earth will worship You, And will sing praises
to You; They will sing praises to Your name.*

—Psalm 66:4

*A church cannot be on mission with God without
an energizing corporate worship experience that
helps the body encounter God's holiness.*

—Jim Herrington, *Leading Congregational Change*

MOST OF US READ the newspaper every morning. Journalists cover a variety of newsworthy stories: international, national, local, social, business, entertainment, sports. Some readers turn to the international and national headlines first. Others begin with local news. Some go straight to the stock market report; others head for game scores and team standings. Most readers can find their favorite section of the newspaper with their eyes closed, because the paper is compiled in the same order every day.

But what if the *news* were the same every day? Same stories. Same stock values. Same scores. Same movies being reviewed. How long would most subscribers maintain their subscription? The newspaper's success depends upon its reporters delivering fresh information, new stories, and more thorough investigation of current events every day.

We enjoy reading newspapers because the form remains consistent while the content changes. The very same formula works for our church experience. Missional churches understand this and rewrite worship every week. They do not deliver the same experience every time they gather for corporate worship. The form is consistent, but the experience is always new.

Many of our churches go through the motions of worship in a way that makes the service more to be endured than enjoyed. The *Westminster Confession* identifies the primary purpose of man "to glorify God and to enjoy Him forever." Certainly, joy is only one emotion that may result from entering His presence, but it challenges the mind to consider encountering God without being touched by some emotion. Can one hold fire and not be burned? Hardly. Neither can the worshiper encounter God without being changed.

Here are the ingredients the missional church uses to make sure worship stays fresh:

- God is the focus of worship.
- Worship is experiential.
- Worship is about content, not form.
- Worship is highly participatory.
- Worship values creativity.
- Worship is more than words.

God Is the Focus of Worship

Worship is designed to exalt God, not to entertain people. Missional congregations are sensitive to communication that enables unchurched people to understand their message, but they are not afraid to include the mysterious or inexplicable in worship. Not every aspect of worship can be understood by one who has never entered relationship with God. As we know, mystery remains even for those who do know God.

We are comfortable with unanswered questions. Life is not all easy answers. Missional communities worship a God who is beyond explanation. He may be experienced, but not explained. He can be encountered, but not controlled. Missional communities invite those who do not yet know God to join experiences of worship, knowing their encounter with God's Spirit might draw them closer to personal relationship with Him. Although it includes those who are not yet disciples, worship is not intended to reach the unreached, but to allow those who know God to bring Him praise.

Missional congregations encounter tensions in worship. One tension develops around the nature of worshipping a God who is both transcendent and immanent. Disciples experience personal intimacy with God and therefore enjoy the closeness of His presence in worship. Yet that closeness does not result in too great familiarity. The same God who is immanent and present—Immanuel, God with us—is also the God beyond. His infinite thoughts and ways are beyond the capacity of finite minds to grasp. He is worshipped as the God with us, and the God beyond us.

Without regard to congregational size, missional communities experience corporate worship as an audience of One. As members worship, they exalt God, explore His glory, and extol relationship with Him among those present. He is the singular focus of worship. Worship is not to entertain those present, nor to offer religious education. Evangelism is not the focus of worship. Neither is worship a self-help session for those attending. Worship is the experience of God's people entering His presence for His benefit.

Worship Is Experiential

Some Protestant traditions refer to worship experiences as "worship services." This stems from the use of the Greek word translated as both "worship" and "service" in the New Testament, *latreuo*. A familiar derivative of the Greek word in English is "liturgy," another designation for worship. Through worship, participants serve God with praise and adoration. Service is a gift.

In other parts of our lives, research reveals that we prefer engaging in experiences rather than passively receiving goods or services. The more immersed and actively involved one is in an experience, the more memorable that experience is.[1] Should church be any different?

Most people would agree that many worship services do not actively engage people. Worshipers sit in pews watching those on the stage (the active participants in the experience). From this perspective, what many call "worship" appears more entertainment than involvement. Authentic worship invites participants, not spectators. Worship is not learning about God; it is encountering God. It is not hearing about Him, but hearing Him. Worship is not standing some distance away and looking on; it is entering His presence. Worship is experiential and participative. It is active. The experience of worship changes us. Worship burns encounter with the Holy deep within the soul.

As missional congregations encounter God and are shaped by His heart, a natural conversation results in which disciples confess their desire to be useful instruments for His purpose. Authentic worship and corporate prayer are simultaneously found in missional churches. The breadth of God's mission would overwhelm disciples were they not able to find new strength through prayer. The models in which corporate prayer is manifested vary, but there is conformity in the significance placed upon prayer. Missional churches are prayer-based congregations.

Antioch Community Church is involved in church planting in more than twenty nations. According to the diverse situations their members face in those countries, the congregation is driven to prayer. Intuitively and experientially, they understand John Piper's statement that "The reason the Father gives the disciples the instrument of prayer is because Jesus has given them a mission."[2] The Antioch Prayer Room has stations encircling the room. Each station hosts current prayer concerns from a nation where Antioch members are involved in church planting. Intercession becomes personal and poignant as members ask God to prepare fellow members for the situations they face, protection from danger, and for unique opportunities through which the Gospel can be communicated.

Jimmy Seibert recalled how the congregation prayed around the clock when Antioch learned of the imprisonment in Ghazni, Afghanistan, of two of their member missionaries, Heather Mercer and Dana Curry, in 2002. Beyond the twenty-four-hour prayer room, Antioch small groups routinely offer twenty to thirty hours per week of prayer meetings throughout the community, as well as all-night prayer events three times a year. As part of worship services Antioch offers ten two-person prayer teams who listen and pray for concerns shared by members and guests. The priority of prayer illustrated through Antioch Community is representative of other missional congregations. Rewriting worship every week translates ongoing, up-to-the-minute prayer as a vital dialogue between God and His missional people. As an element of corporate worship, their prayer is neither routine nor simple formality.

Worship Is About Content, Not Form

Today, battles are being waged over the propriety of changing traditions in worship. Enormous energy is invested in advocating for particular forms of worship. Churches debate the use of traditional hymns and contemporary praise choruses, formality or informality. Ultimately, such debate may reveal the egocentric perception of worship held by those involved. These worship wars are a vivid evidence of focus on the "consumer" rather than the One who inhabits praise. In the long history of worship, God has been pleased to accept diverse expressions, so long as those involved in worship are singularly focused upon Him.

Some interpret the missional church as synonymous with contemporary forms of worship. This assumption is false. Missional congregations are worshipping through traditional and contemporary expressions, singing hymns and praise songs, reading from the King James Version as well as The Message. Some are liturgical, some charismatic. Whether through traditional or contemporary expressions, their worship celebrates personal relationship with God: the Father, the Son, and the Holy Spirit.

People frequently maintain traditions long beyond their contemporary relevance without explanation of their previous meaning. In *Full Circle*, Michael Palin recalls his encounter with an eighth-generation Japanese restaurant owner in Tokyo, who every day lays three piles of salt out in the street: "Mr. Watanabe is punctilious in observing tradition. . . . [Putting salt in the street] dates back to the time when people traveled into town with their cows. When they found salt the cows would always stop to lick it up, giving their owners time to size up the restaurant."[3] The time is long past when cows accompanied their owners through the city streets of Tokyo, and there is no logical rationale for placing salt outside a restaurant door. But traditions possess undercurrents that continue to pull others into their powerful influence and observance. Salt is faithfully piled on the sidewalks of Tokyo, although few know the reason. Most would identify the act as a waste, but for Mr. Watanabe it is not waste. It is tradition. Traditions are not bad, in a restaurant or worship; they simply require explanation for those who are unable to grasp their significance.

If traditions are not bad, neither is innovation necessarily good. In his *Letters to Malcolm*, C. S. Lewis despaired over innovative priests who seemed obligated to bring in new forms of liturgy. People, said Lewis, go to church to "enact" the service, not to be entertained: "Every service is a structure of acts and words. . . . And it . . . 'works' best . . . when, through long familiarity, we don't have to think about it. . . . The perfect church service would be one we were almost unaware of; our attention would have been on God."[4]

When innovation takes the focus off God and forces participants to focus instead on the acts of worship, it reduces worship to something less. Worship is encounter with God. Missional churches are committed to that experience without regard to innovation or tradition. The form must serve the focus, and the focus of worship is God.

Some missional communities offer multiple services in different worship formats and find that members frequently move between those services. Mosaic's morning worship in a high school auditorium tends to be more experimental, including all sorts of elements from service to service: high-energy praise, band, dance, drama, an artist rendering the message on canvas, and video. An evening worship service is held in a nightclub facility in downtown Los Angeles. Reflecting on the services, lead pastor Erwin McManus explained: "There is no traditional service, or contemporary service. They are all expressive of the environment that is there. So, the Sunday morning service was usually the most rock kind of hard edge service, which kind of would shock people. The nightclub was really, in our mind, the more straightforward. And part of it is because we walked into a nightclub and said, 'OK, we pretty much hit the relevant section of our approach, but we need to create the quiet sacred.' "[5]

In fact, both are sacred; but one tends to be more high-energy, while the other invites a more contemplative response. Mosaic finds members seeking both because spirituality is dynamic. Sometimes the soul hungers for quiet, and sometimes a sacred shout to the Lord. Traditional in form one moment; writing new traditions in another. Rewriting worship every week breathes new life into the old and creates sacred space for the new.

Worship Is Highly Participatory

Worship has often been described as the most consumer-oriented aspect of Western Christianity. A handful of "leaders" prepare and carry out services, while the majority of those attending sit and observe. In this environment it is difficult to avoid the sense of entertainment rather than participation. Congregations are spectators watching others worship, rather than actors on stage bringing their own sacrifice of praise to God. In missional communities, inclusion of members in the act of worship is critical. They actively seek maximum involvement of members in planning, preparing, and expressing worship. Many of those aspects of involvement are not unique to missional churches, but the cumulative effect of their ongoing inclusion of members is distinct.

Visit Fellowship Bible Church, and members guide you to designated guest parking areas. You are greeted as you step from your vehicle by another helpful member who directs you to the worship center, to an appropriate class, or to the area where child care is available. Enter the facility and still other members identify themselves, welcome you (indi-cating their enthusiastic expectation that you will enjoy the worship), pro-vide printed information about Fellowship Bible Church, and help you find your way. Guests encounter members staffing various displays of information on upcoming events or ongoing ministries. Before ever enter-ing the worship service, with its high member involvement, the guest gets the sense that every member of Fellowship Bible Church has a task.

Bob Roberts values the input of members in preparing worship. The unique gifts and talents of members may be employed months in advance of a given service, in writing dramatic presentations, developing multi-media, composing new music, or preparing NorthWood Notes (thematic devotional guides enabling members to reflect weekdays upon subjects being addressed in weekly worship). Roberts's goal for worship is "not a slick show, but creation of an atmosphere for worship, a 'barometric pressure' where God can be encountered." Creating that environment does not occur without attentive involvement of a large contingent of gifted members.

As members are involved, one can often sense profound emotion related to their personal roles. The Church of the Resurrection in Lea-wood, Kansas, invites all who know Christ as Savior to participate in Communion. In a sanctuary filled with some eighteen hundred members and guests, the logistics of serving the elements is a significant challenge. The process they have adopted is not only efficient in serving a large num-ber of congregants; it affords an intense experience in which members serve one another. As the minister invites personal preparation to receive communion, pairs of members, many husbands and wives, emerge from around the facility and make their way to designated serving locations. By their placement, the sanctuary is divided into sections allowing all par-ticipants to be served in less than eight minutes. The process allows an orderly flow as individuals pass by those serving the elements. From a loaf of bread, the server tears a portion and gives it to each communicant, say-ing "This is the Body of Christ broken for you." The second server then guides the participant in dipping the bread into a common cup. Her words might include, "This cup is the blood of Christ offered for your redemp-tion. Accept these in remembrance of Christ's gift of love for you."

In both instances, members are served by fellow members in a personal manner. Observing the solemnity of the service, one frequently notices tears streaming down the faces of the servers and those being served. The method of distribution is not unique to Church of the Resurrection, but the deep pathos clearly shared among members in the experience affirms the significance as these members exercise leadership in worship.

Worship Values Creativity

The high value of member gifts and talents is closely associated with a high level of member participation in worship in missional churches. Traditionally, evangelical churches in the West have placed priority on proclamation through sermons and choral music. Today, missional communities are refocusing worship to include other communicative techniques. Chris Seay, pastor of Ecclesia, a missional community in Houston, is a second-generation pastor. Just as he is different from his father, so is his perception of worship. "We believe that artists are our current day preachers and storytellers," he told *Christianity Today,* "so we do things through visual art and film and literature that we couldn't do otherwise. We believe that's the best way to tell the story of God."[6]

Seay's high view of creative arts is typical of other missional leaders. Mosaic is located in Los Angeles, a primary hub of artistic creativity, so it's not surprising that this community places importance upon creativity. "We really do see God as an artist who uses the human spirit as His canvas. We have a really high view of human creativity," says Mosaic's Erwin McManus. "What does it mean that God has placed His image and likeness inside of us? We almost try to eliminate any reality of human capacity. We say things like, when something good happens, 'It wasn't me, it was the Lord.' Whenever something bad happens, 'It wasn't the Lord, it was me.' It seems we are incapable of understanding that God created us to do good. It seems we don't really understand that our greatest capacity is the result of being created by God. You honor God by living the way you were designed and using the gifts he gave you."

It is this attitude that empowers the creativity of their worship experience. McManus explains: "Not everyone can paint, or sculpt, or dance, but everyone is creative. Most people say, 'Oh, I'm not creative.' What they mean is they are not artistic. What we have to help them realize is that creativity spans the whole human experience. You can be creative through mercy or through administration, or creative through giving or teaching."[7]

Mosaic invites members and guests to use their creativity in serving God. Their worship reflects a host of different media through which the message of the Gospel is communicated. As a guest in worship, one might first be overwhelmed at the technical skills furnished by members. Before worship, they transform the high school auditorium into a high-tech worship center capable of video, sound, and lighting with quality rivaling that of any theater. Other team members use plants, tables, chairs, couches, and artwork to make hallways comfortable and informal gathering spaces. Their attention to interior design must be successful, because people gather and mingle at length before and after worship.

Entering the worship celebration, one immediately recognizes that the auditorium pulsates with sounds from the Mosaic band; but Mosaic uses all kinds of creative expression—not just voices—in praise. For example, a well-choreographed dance group might interpret the theme around which the celebration of the day is planned. The message may also incorporate the pastor's speaking, video segments, and original drama written and acted by Mosaic members. At the outset of the sermon, an artist, prominently visible at the front of the room, might begin interpreting the message with acrylic paints on a blank canvas.

Here's how one such experience went: In an April 2002 series, "Awakening the Human Spirit," the sermon focused on "Loving the Lord with All Your Strength." During that message, an artist named Noami systematically developed a highlighted background on canvas. Gradually, her strokes revealed a wooden cross with the outline of a human form superimposed upon it. As the message reiterated implications of loving God with all one's strength, the artist revealed one hand of the image holding tightly to one side of the cross. At the last moment, the painting was completed, with the victim's other arm shown flexing in a display of muscular strength. Whether those present remembered words spoken during the message, the impression of the artists' rendering brought tears to many eyes. The painting prompted reflections: "Although Christ's hands were nailed to the cross, it was not nails that held Him there. Christ's sacrificial death was not that of a victim after all. His death was the ultimate display of His will to love with all His strength." Without the creativity of the artist, the message would have missed another window to the soul.

The Mosaic experience is not for everyone. A look at other churches shows that there is an infinite variety of ways in which creativity can be expressed. There is no "right way." A number of communities compose songs to personalize praise and worship. Where these practices are the norm, congregations frequently have the opportunity to "sing a new song to the Lord" (Psalm 33:3). To assist members in learning new songs, churches produce and distribute CDs or audiotapes. They are also used to facilitate meaningful personal worship as members listen and join in singing praise in their homes or automobiles. Although not always studio-quality in their production, some are excellent and all perform a valuable function and enhance worship. Commenting on a CD written and produced by one of the worship bands of Christ Fellowship, Jamye said, "One of their songs was nominated for a Dove Award. These guys are good. But they are not 'in it' to get rich or famous. Their desire is simply to give praise to the Father."

Not all creative expression in worship involves the arts. A totally different invitation to worship was extended members of Christ Church Episcopal in Overland Park, Kansas. This announcement was made at the conclusion of a morning worship service: "Next Saturday morning you are invited to worship at 9:00 A.M. with spades, compost, and bedding plants as we care for Christ Church Gardens." Maintaining the beauty of a prayer garden is, for these individuals, an act of worship. One member of the congregation commented, "Sometimes I sense God's presence more as we work together, sometimes singing, often quiet, than I do in the formal service." Missional communities value the creative gifting of disciples and use those gifts in rewriting worship every week.

Worship Is More Than Words

Perhaps the Western church has become too verbal for its own good. In a culture experiencing information overload, an archaic truth is being remembered: intense impact can be achieved through silence. Missional communities seek to gain the hearing of those who do not know Christ. In a noisy culture, it is interesting to note the impact of a quiet coffee shop adorned with Christian symbols, open to the public. Churches are exploring the potential truth found in the words of Michael Riddell: "I have gradually been moving towards the conclusion that our words are getting in the way of the gospel—that the church is somehow imprisoned in a kind of cognitive captivity which is inhibiting our mission, maybe even keeping Christ on the fringes."[8]

In New York City's Union Square Park, following the tragedy of September 11, 2001, visitors placed hundreds of candles in symbolic gestures of concern for those killed. Early one evening, as a chaplain mingled with people in the park, inviting them to tell their own stories and offering prayer, he noticed a woman relighting one candle after another. She had taken it upon herself to keep the flames burning. Although she was not a Christian, her actions were motivated by a deep spiritual longing. She said, "I am not a religious person. For me, this *is* my prayer, to keep the candles lit." Her story should remind churches that spirituality is more than words.

Author John Drane has wrestled with the church's struggle for relevant communication. He sounds a prophetic note related to his wife's method of communicating the Gospel, silent mime: "Olive decided the time was right to invite her audiences to join her in having crosses painted on their eyes so that they could, quite literally, in her words 'see the world the way God sees it—through the cross.'"[9]

Missional churches are seeking to provide worship in ways that allow every person to experience God meaningfully and authentically. Some are rushing into the future by reclaiming quiet old forms of worship. Others employ multimedia, dance, and drama. Worship forms are as diverse as the communication techniques embraced by those who follow God and seek to be shaped by His heart.

Reflection and Application

1. Reflect on corporate worship experiences that have been most meaningful to you. Which components resulted in profound impact upon you? Could those components be integrated into your church's worship? How?

2. Invite members to a small-group discussion. Ask to write their responses to these phrases, and then ask them to discuss the responses:

- Sometimes I wish worship would include . . .
- The part of our worship experience that often annoys me is . . .
- If I were asked to lead in worship, I would offer to . . .

3. How does your church prepare individuals and families for personal worship? What could you do to enhance this preparation?

4. Schedule, within the next three months, a personal worship retreat of at least one day. In preparation for the retreat, review and select a retreat guide for use in that experience.

SUGGESTED READING

Black, K. *Culturally-Conscious Worship*. St. Louis, Mo.: Chalice Press, 2000.
Job, R. P. *A Guide to Retreat for All God's Shepherds*. Nashville, Tenn.: Abingdon Press, 1994.

Missional Practice Assessment

Rate each statement that follows from 1 (the statement is not true of our church) to 7 (the statement is true of our church) by circling the appropriate response. The greatest insight will be gained if you avoid selecting 4 as a response. Please use that selection minimally. When you are finished, transfer your responses to the assessments in the Appendix and total your scores to find your net response. Your group's response to these assessments gives a clear picture of your church's readiness to move to being missional.

Our worship focuses on an audience of one.

1   2   3   4   5   6   7

We use a team of members in planning worship.

1   2   3   4   5   6   7

Members lead corporate worship through sharing their various talents.

1   2   3   4   5   6   7

We routinely incorporate new ideas or methods in worship.

1   2   3   4   5   6   7

We challenge members to be responsible in their obedience to God.

1   2   3   4   5   6   7

Our worship is designed to use each of the five senses.

1   2   3   4   5   6   7

Our church prepares members for personal worship experiences.

1   2   3   4   5   6   7

MISSIONAL PRACTICE NUMBER FIVE

LIVE APOSTOLICALLY

---

*Of the sons of Issachar, men who understood the times,
with knowledge of what Israel would do, their chiefs were
two hundred; and all their kinsmen were at their command.*

—1 Chronicles 12:32

*Only Jesus Christ, who bids us follow him, knows the
journey's end. But we do know that it will be a road
of boundless mercy. Discipleship means joy.*

—Dietrich Bonhoeffer, *The Cost of Discipleship*

LEROY EIMS IS a marvelous disciple builder, author, and master storyteller who called for authentic discipleship in the twentieth century as a representative of the Navigators. Some years ago, as he tells the story, he was listening to the radio while driving toward his Colorado Springs home. It was Saturday evening, and he was listening to sounds of the Big Band era. While enjoying one of his favorites, "Chattanooga Choo-Choo," the song was suddenly drowned out by a higher-powered station broadcasting a "fire and brimstone" preacher who shouted, "Repent. Repent, now!" In response to this appeal, Eims replied, "Now my problem is I've already done that. I did that years ago. I *have* repented. Right now, I am trying to listen to 'Chattanooga Choo-Choo'! But he won't let me listen to 'Chattanooga Choo-Choo'; instead he insists that I repent!"

Living apostolically can be like that. Our connection to the church can be so strong that it repeatedly interrupts our attempts to move beyond the church and into the culture of the world. While we try to hear what is being said in the world, the sounds of our religious traditions continue to overpower us. Our attempts to bridge the span from the church into the world prove difficult and are likely to be replete with accusations of compromise. Some Christian leaders fear the effect secular influences may have upon the disciple, so they promote isolation from those influences.

Ecclesia's Chris Seay recounts a refrain familiar to many evangelicals. "I remember being sixteen years old and being taught . . . 'Stay away from culture . . . your brain is a sponge, you'll absorb whatever you hear and see.' I began to study Scripture and I read passages like that in Daniel, where Daniel was educated by sorcerers, magicians, pagan priests, and astrologers. It says at the end of chapter one that he became ten times wiser in those things than the people that taught him. . . . Scripture was his guide through all of the mess of his own pagan culture that I find to be very similar to our culture."[1]

Although some advocate avoiding the world's cultural influences, the fact is, Christians are sent into the world. Some speak of the separation of sacred and spiritual cultures. The distinction poses major problems for the missional church, since it intimates only "church" activities as spiritual. For followers of Christ, the Spirit is always present as they move beyond stained glass and pews into office buildings and theaters. Missional churches believe every follower of Christ is one who is sent. All are missionaries. Therefore missional churches seek to prepare members to live apostolically.

Author Craig Van Gelder says, "In being missional by nature, local congregations seek to reach beyond themselves into their local areas to bear witness to the reign of God and to invite others into the community of faith." He goes on to say that they must "learn the language of faith because they are created by the Spirit. But they are also responsible to learn the language of their specific settings because they are contextual."[2]

Missional communities speak two languages: the language of the Body and the language of the world. Among the first activities of missionaries appointed to serve in international environments has traditionally been language school. Value has been placed upon the capacity to communicate in the vernacular of the people. Today, members of missional churches must be bilingual in that they must be able to communicate in terms that can be understood by those without as well as those within the church.

What does it mean to live apostolically? In this book, my use of the term implies certain characteristics. First, every disciple of Christ is "one who is sent" into the world. Second, the term implies the church lives in a culture more similar to the first century than different from it. Finally, the church is tasked with equipping disciples to interpret contemporary cultures and engage them in dialogue that magnifies Christ. Disciples are integrated in the world, yet distinct from the world as Kingdom citizens.

People in missional communities live apostolically in these ways:

- They live apostolically as those sent.
- They live mission in a neo-apostolic era.
- Apostolic living shares good news.

They Live Apostolically as Those Sent

A person who does not believe every disciple of Jesus Christ is sent by Him into the world rejects the essence of the missional church. The person must then believe that only select ones are sent by Christ on mission. This ideology has been reinforced, probably unwittingly, by denominational entities and mission-sending agencies.

We have frequently heard about the work of missionaries around the world. We have been asked to pray for those whom God has sent and for those among whom they are seeking to share the Gospel. We have been asked to give financially so that those who were called to missions would be able to go and serve. Most church budgets include a portion of every dollar received sent to the support of missionaries. Conventional churches with missions programs have often provided age-level education introducing missionaries supported through those financial gifts. Upon return from their place of service, missionaries have been invited to show slides and artifacts while they tell supporting churches about the mission work in which they are involved. These mission experiences are critical and have resulted in millions coming to know Christ as Savior. But it is also true that some disciples have been left with the impression that praying and giving totally fulfills their mission responsibility.

Scripture, however, relates the role of all followers as witnesses pointing others to acknowledge God. In the Old Testament, God blessed those who followed Him in order that they might be a blessing to the nations (Genesis 12:3). He longed that His place of worship would be called a house of prayer for all the nations (Isaiah 56:7). There the longing of God was that all the nations worship Him (Psalm 96:3; 103:22). It was for that purpose that He chose a people who would extol His name among the nations. The New Testament echoes the heart of God reflected in the Old Testament. The incarnation is the central image showing the heart of God and His desire to draw men unto Himself. Jesus was sent into the world to seek and to save the lost. Before He returned to heaven, He commissioned His church in the continuation of His missional purpose (John 20:21; Matthew 28:18–20; Acts 1:8). The apostolic sending of disciples is woven through the entire scriptural account.

The use of the term *apostolic* is not intended to convey any line of succession with those originally called "apostles." Scholars have written extensively reflecting on the term's origins, its use by various writers in the New Testament, and whether the term was limited to the original twelve disciples (with the addition of Paul) or to a larger group of individuals whose primary task was mission and upon whose ministry the early church was founded. The term is used here to denote the *kind of task* given to all followers of Christ. All Christians are called into personal relationship with Him and are sent into the world to witness His saving grace among those who have not confessed Him as Lord. The continuing apostolic function of the Body of Christ may be derived from Christ's prayer for "all those who will believe" (John 17:13–21), from the continuing nature of the commission given to the Church (Matthew 28:18–20; Luke 24:46–48; Acts 1:8), and is implicit since the return of Christ awaits completion of Gospel proclamation among all people groups (Matthew 24:14). Those who have experienced intimacy with Christ are commanded to be witnesses among those who have not known Him.

Roy Fish and J. E. Conant explain the missional task of all believers in *Every Member Evangelism for Today* as "a personal command to every Christian to . . . seek to win every lost individual in his personal world to salvation. We are also to scatter over the inhabited earth, as the providence of God leads and opens the way, so that the whole world will be continuously and simultaneously evangelized."[3]

This apostolic task is the temporal purpose of the church, just as it was in the first century. Although its eternal purpose is to worship God and enjoy Him forever, its temporal purpose is to proclaim His glory among the nations in order that people from every nation may join to worship Him. Since every believer is to bear witness, is sent to evidence the veracity of the Gospel message, every believer is on mission. Injustice is done to the term *missionary* when it is reserved only for professional or vocational ministry personnel who cross oceans or other geographical boundaries in their assignment. Missionaries are ones who are sent, and for the New Testament church that includes every believer. All disciples are to live apostolically.

Among the most poignant implications of this lifestyle is the movement away from self and toward another. It is a lifestyle that involves placing the need of another above one's own desire. It is sacrificial and service-oriented; it can be uncomfortable, and it is not always safe. This missional lifestyle, like the incarnation of Christ, may include movement across barriers and into disparate cultures. It finds pattern in the Acts 10 account in which Peter accepted the mission of going to the home of one whom his culture identified as unclean. Obedience to the mission required relinquishing any prerogative of judgment, calling unclean what God deems clean. For the missional disciple, mission is not geographical but philosophical. It is not defined by the location to which the disciple goes, nor the number of oceans crossed in the process, but rather by the disciple's message demonstrated and declared through an incarnational lifestyle.

Michael Riddell says that "leaving our place of security, to travel to the place where others are . . . is the heartbeat of the incarnation, the movement of God outward into the creation to stand with us in Jesus. This hour of crisis in the West calls for such thinking outside the box. . . ."4 Outside-the-box thinking characterizes missional communities. As people sent by God into His world to share His good news of grace and hope, one of their abandoned boxes is retreat from the world into an isolated existence. Missional communities forge into the world, abandoning their comfort zone, accompanied by the Comforter.

They Live Mission in a Neo-Apostolic Era

Under the leadership of Robert Lewis, Fellowship Bible Church has left the security of former ways and risked asking questions about the contemporary society in which it ministers. Lewis identifies the importance of understanding the context in which mission takes place: "As an engineer of bridges between the church and the world, it is the responsibility of the church leader to understand . . . the spirit and forces of the age. . . . The very life of the church is intertwined with a recognition of the times. I am fearful that by clinging to what is cherished or what seems successful, many pastors and/or their church boards refuse to embrace what is vital."5

His words parallel those used to describe the sons of Issachar as "men who understood the times, with knowledge of what Israel should do . . ." (1 Chronicles 12:32). Luke recorded, of King David, that "after he had served the purpose of God in his own generation, [he] fell asleep, and was laid among his fathers . . ." (Acts 13:36). In every generation, God raises new leaders who forge into their social environment with firm foundations in the unchanging counsel of God. They understand the unique environment into which they are sent on mission, and they serve the eternal God effectively in the same. Contemporary images are interpreted through historic truths.

Chris Seay believes the arts hold great potential as a source through which church leaders gain insight into the times. Some refuse to see or hear productions of the entertainment industry; Seay believes church leaders must attend such images (although he acknowledges the challenge of finding the right level of engagement): "In music and movies, you see all of these deep spiritual questions. And the people that are supposed to engage those questions have removed themselves. We pull away from culture to the point where we can no longer affect it."[6]

Those seeking to understand the times are also aware that images of the arts are no longer simply regional or national. Mission is accomplished in a global environment where media allows simultaneous access to experiences. Culture is "real-time" oriented. To be relevant to those in their context, church leaders must be able to respond with Godly counsel to current events. The luxury of waiting days to develop a response to global events is past. Understanding the times cannot be the task of a few who subsequently interpret experiences for others. Church leaders must be able to respond in real time as their constituents are exposed to cultural events.

Brian McLaren, pastor of Cedar Ridge Community Church, in the Washington, D.C.–Baltimore area, uses segments from current movies each year in his popular message series "God in the Movies." Instead of using these images to point out contemporary decadence, he does something different: "I look for moments of 'glory' in the films and trace that glory to its source in the Creator. . . . Film has become . . . a kind of universal language, and people appreciate it when we take the time to learn their culture and exegete it with respect, not disdain."[7]

Like McLaren, missional leaders invest the time necessary to know the culture in which they live and treat it respectfully. This is not to imply tolerance without standards, but it does assume the ability to read statements of spiritual hunger and creative fiat, reflections of the Creator's image stamped upon every individual, in the vernacular of contemporary cultures. Greater proficiency in hearing the spiritual cries verbalized in various genres results in enhanced sensitivity to respond with spiritual counsel that bridges the chasm from seeker to disciple.

The apostolic church in a neo-apostolic era must confront the cultural contexts of its age. George Hunter has helped the Western church grasp

additional implications of being apostolic, and he has identified four components marking first-century apostolic churches that coincide with some
of the missional practices we have seen: (1) they believe God has sent them
to reach the unchurched, (2) the heart of their message and theology is
the gospel of early apostolic Christianity, (3) they adapt their message to
the language and culture of the people they want to reach, and (4) they
incorporate key features of early apostolic Christianity.[8]

The culture in which missional churches are growing is filled with
masses of people seeking a spiritual gyroscope to bring a sense of order
to their personal experiences and world events. Conventional churches
continue focusing ministry on care for their members, seemingly unaware
of or unconcerned for the masses who constitute this generation's potential spiritual harvest. More unreached people are alive today than any
time in church history, yet too few Christians practice missional lifestyles,
invite others to journey toward knowing God, and validate through
actions their status as "new creatures in Christ." The harvest is plentiful;
the laborers are few.

Apostolic Living Shares Good News

Missional disciples share Christ naturally, inviting people to embark on
a lifelong journey toward intimacy with God. Their methods of sharing
the Good News of Christ tend not to be confrontational and propositional. They feel that sharing Christ is best accomplished in the natural
dialogue that develops between friends. It is helping friends begin moving toward God.

Investing in a long dialogue with a nonbeliever is not nearly as easy as
presenting a memorized "plan of salvation." These "plans" generally
employ propositional truths, spiritual laws, that are communicated
together with selected verses of scripture. In this personal evangelism
method, one introduces truths and invites the hearer to respond. The
response paves the way for an on-the-spot acceptance or rejection of relationship with God. After a few minutes listening to a presentation, the
decision is made. The person making the presentation has fulfilled his or
her evangelistic responsibility and can move on to witness to the next can-
didate. The method is not nearly as messy as getting involved in listening
to people as they struggle, and letting them see that we struggle too. Or
crying with them in their pain, or walking beside them as they seek
answers to the tough situations of life. Simply sharing the message without
investing in the stuff of their everyday lives is much easier. I wonder, is
that what it really means to share the Good News? Is sharing simply

about information? Or is it about incarnation? Does one share authentically without entering into the life of the other?

At New Heights Church, Matt Hannan and his staff are equipping
members to share Christ in ways that embrace individuals wherever they
are in their journey toward God. Rather than teaching presentations of
propositional truths, they are teaching people to ask questions, listen, and
bless people where they are. Using concepts developed by James Engel
and Viggo Soogard, New Heights helps disciples understand the various
stages in the pilgrimage through which people pass in coming to mature
faith. The process, sometimes called the Engel scale, examines the spiritual decision process.

The scale assumes a communicator of the Gospel, response of one with
whom the Gospel is being communicated, and the activity of God in
drawing people to himself. Engel describes the scale as showing "various
stages in the pilgrimage, starting from no background or awareness of the
Christian faith, moving through conversion and on into a lifelong pattern
of growth and maturity as a Christian."[9]

Applying Engel's scale in apostolic evangelism, Hannan explained to
me how it might be used in a model scenario:

> Let's assume I am meeting with a man who has been attending church
> for a while, maybe just to please his wife. When we meet I might
> begin by saying, "You know, I am glad we got this chance. I have
> looked forward to the opportunity just to get to know you a little
> bit." After we spend some time talking I might say, "Look, at some
> point you are going to expect a little bit of 'God stuff' from me. My
> guess is you are probably not totally alienated from spiritual things,
> but it's not my job to put the arm on you. I can do this for you, that
> may be helpful. I can help you spot yourself on a spiritual road map,
> because if you know where you are on the map, you can decide what
> direction you want to go."
>
> We use a little thing called a spiritual continuum. Drawing a line
> and marking on it I would say, "There's a line here, this mark means
> birth, and this mark means death. I think you are on the line some-
> where." He would probably laugh. "Maybe we could just divide it in
> a couple of different ways. Maybe you are at the point where you are
> just simply spiritually curious. You might be asking things like, 'Is
> there a God?' or 'Is there not a God?' Or 'Is there any spiritual reality
> out there? Is this world the whole thing?' If that's where you are, that's
> a great place to be—it's important. It might be that you have come to
> the point where you are processing spiritual things." When that hap-

pens, I find that people's questions get more specific. They start asking things like "Is the Bible God's Word?" "If God is so good, why did my little sister die when she was five?" Those kinds of things. What I find is when people do that, when they ask more specific questions, they are surprised because they get very distinct answers.

If a person makes it to that point, then the next place for them is focused commitment, a genuine commitment they make. That is why I draw a cross above the line and say "You might say you are on this side of the cross, trusting your own capacities and abilities? Or perhaps you have made the grand decision to be on the other side trusting the work of Christ? If you made that one, it may be that you are here on the line, the place where you are just beginning to take different growth steps." As we talk through the different positions on the continuum I will at some point ask, "Where do you think you are on the map?"

This allows the person to self-identify his position. What I can then do is bless them where they are, offering to help them move to the next place on their spiritual map. This rather than a mentality of witness that says, "Look, either you are in or you are out. I can only bless you if you are on this side." Frankly what is often meant is, "I will only really love you and relate to you if you are on this side." I don't want to do that. So, instead, someone can say to me, "I am just here," or they can start asking other questions. Either way, I can bless them. Knowing where they are is good.

My missionary posture says there are a bunch of issues they have to deal with to come into my world view of spiritual things. I have to allow them time to process those very basic questions. And so I just bless them. And I get to bless them at every point in the process.[10]

Using Engel's scale or other tools in apostolic evangelization does not lessen the importance of the disciple's knowledge of Scripture or the nature of conversion. Tools permit a dialogue-oriented process that values where any individual is in the spiritual-decision process. A natural outgrowth of such dialogue is encouragement in the journey toward greater knowledge of God. At its core, apostolic evangelization assumes leading persons to faith as a relational process rather than a single event.

As missional churches help their members live apostolically, they expect members to invite other people to experience faith in Christ. Bob Duran, a staff member of Mosaic, recounted the story of counsel he gave to a fellow member who was contemplating leaving the community in response to a personality conflict. He told the man, "Just because you are upset over this, do you think God is through using you here at Mosaic? Do you honestly think that it will please Him if you leave? How many people has He allowed you to bring to faith in Him during the last year? Seventy-five or eighty? Then how can you think it is all right for you to leave?"

A member leading seventy-five or eighty people to faith in Christ was not unusual for Mosaic; it was expected. It was just one bit of evidence among the many Bob mentioned. Spiritual reproduction is a natural process in missional churches. Those individuals within a member's own sphere of influence make up their primary mission field. Since every member is a missionary, each understands that he or she is sent into a particular realm in which there is primary evangelistic responsibility. (The next chapter offers more insight into the concept of the primary mission field.)

To live apostolically, one must spend time getting to know lost people. Churches cannot expect members to develop authentic relationships with lost persons if the church continuously asks members to give every discretionary hour in their agenda to church activities. Sometimes members need to be free to hear the "Chattanooga Choo-Choo" being played out in the lives of their friends and neighbors. When Robert Lewis and the leaders of Fellowship Bible Church determined to be a church of irresistible influence in their community, they found that "We didn't need to be more religious; we needed to be more *connected*." Living apostolically means connecting with people who do not know Christ, bringing them Good News.

As the Gospel is presented and validated through the lives of apostolic disciples, it accomplishes wonderful results. The result of every witness is the prerogative of God's Spirit, but missional churches regularly celebrate new lives born into the Kingdom of God. Members are living as those sent, sharing the difference that God is making in their lives, and seeing friends, relatives, neighbors, and work associates join the Kingdom journey.

Reflection and Application

1. Discuss lifestyle implications involved in the statement "Incarnation is always away from self and toward another." How could your church better prepare disciples for an incarnational lifestyle?

2. Enlist members to ask unchurched friends one of these questions, recording the responses: "What spiritual concern do you think most people wonder about?" or "What evidence supports the statement, 'All people are spiritual beings'?" Discuss the responses they bring back.

3. Assess the highest manifestations of creativity and outside-the-box thinking in your congregation during the last twelve months. Did you meet new people through those efforts? Seek to identify population segments in your city with which your church has little or no relationship. Create an "outside the box" strategy for connecting with those people groups.

SUGGESTED READING

Ogden, G. *Unfinished Business: Returning the Ministry to the People of God.* Grand Rapids, Mich.: Zondervan, 2003.

Thompson, W. O. *Concentric Circles of Concern: Seven Stages for Making Disciples.* (rev. and updated by C. V. King.) Nashville, Tenn.: Broadman and Holman, 1999.

Tinsley, W. *The Jesus Encounter: Stories of People in the Bible Who Met Jesus.* Grand Rapids, Mich.: Zondervan, 2002.

Missional Practice Assessment

Rate each statement that follows from 1 (the statement is not true of our church) to 7 (the statement is true of our church) by circling the appropriate response. The greatest insight will be gained if you avoid selecting 4 as a response. Please use that selection minimally. When you are finished, transfer your responses to the assessments in the Appendix and total your scores to find your net response. Your group's response to these assessments gives a clear picture of your church's readiness to move to being missional.

Our members consider themselves as missionaries.

1   2   3   4   5   6   7

Members routinely introduce new believers to faith in Christ.

1   2   3   4   5   6   7

Members interpret contemporary culture through Biblical guidance.

1   2   3   4   5   6   7

We encourage members to participate in "secular" social groups.

1   2   3   4   5   6   7

Our church is transforming the community in which we live.

1   2   3   4   5   6   7

Members learn to establish and maintain authentic relationships with lost persons.

1   2   3   4   5   6   7

Members are involved in leading the nations to worship Christ.

1   2   3   4   5   6   7

8

MISSIONAL PRACTICE NUMBER SIX

EXPECT TO CHANGE THE WORLD

---

*. . . but you will receive power when the Holy Spirit
has come upon you; and you shall be My witnesses
both in Jerusalem, and in all Judea and Samaria,
and even to the remotest part of the earth.*

—Acts 1:8

*It is still God's policy to work through the embarrassingly
insignificant to change his world and create his future.*

—Tom Sine, *The Mustard Seed Conspiracy*

THE POINT OF THE KINGDOM is transformation. God is radically transforming disciples who can manifest the effect of His reign through their lives
(Romans 12:2). Missional churches expect to transform the world through
involvement and ministry. Beginning with their own city, they extend their
focus to their state, their nation, and the ends of the earth. They believe
the Gospel is still the power of God to transform all who believe.

Many church members say they believe their churches possess something that can potentially transform the world. Often, however, the words remain rhetoric. When pressed, members admit their sense of isolation from the world, acknowledging their existence has minimal influence within their own community, much less beyond. They gather from week to week and go through the motions, but they are in maintenance mode. They do not actually believe they possess the power or influence required to change the world. They are holding on, rather than storming ahead; isolated from the world rather than engaged in changing it. They have forgotten that the first-century church began with only a handful of disciples. The Holy Spirit who empowered them is the same Spirit at work in the church today. He has not abdicated His position of authority nor lost any of His power.

We can see examples of a small group making a huge impact in the secular realm. During the early 1980s, Steve Jobs's upstart young Apple company was not given odds to succeed by the monolith, IBM. But as one Apple insider later said, "[our] fundamental purpose was to innovate, invent, and lead an entire cultural revolution. . . . All the people I met there, passionate young people, truly believed they were changing the world, not selling computers."[1] Surely employees of a computer company possess no greater capacity to effect world change than does the Body of Christ, indwelt and empowered by God's dynamic Spirit.

Churches are rediscovering God's purpose: that all the nations have opportunity to know Him and gather in praise of His glory. Missional congregations are calling disciples to live as missionaries, whose primary task is inviting others to journey as followers of Christ. They believe, through faith, all things are possible. Like Bob Roberts, at NorthWood Church for the Communities, they have heard God's probing question: "What would it look like for a church to turn the world upside down today?" That was the world's assessment concerning the impact of a few disciples in Acts 17. If it could be said then, why not today?

Missional churches such as NorthWood are seeking to be that kind of church. They are not just preparing people for eternity; they are equipping and deploying disciples for world impact now. NorthWood, playing on a popular media advertisement, challenges members to their own rendition of "MLife": missional living. They believe the Kingdom that accomplishes inner transformation in disciples will result in external transformation of the world. Their commitment is to be an instrument through which God can turn the world upside down. They expect to change the world.

When I interviewed him on the purpose of New Heights Church, Matt Hannan responded, "New Heights wants to be a church that makes a difference on earth for heaven's sake. The point is," he continued, "if you can not see the difference on earth, then it does not matter what you are doing for heaven's sake. If our focus is only to save souls, we are missing our opportunity. If our focus is just to minister to the body, we are missing our opportunity. We have to unite the two." New Heights has effectively united the two components of evangelization, declaration and demonstration. The church has a transformational social impact among residents in Vancouver, Washington, and profound spiritual impact as new disciples begin the journey to follow Christ. They expect to change the world.

Mosaic's ultimate criterion for determining its effectiveness is the transformation of Los Angeles. Erwin McManus discussed their expectation to effect change: "We want to see people's lives changed, individually, one by one, and we want to see that change affecting their families, communities, and social structures. Whether it's their business place, their career, or whatever, it will be changed. We expect impact as more people are coming to faith in Jesus Christ and becoming sincere and revolutionary followers of Him. We also expect their companies will change the way they do business and the way they act toward each other, whether the movie industry or other corporate segments." Indeed, McManus believes the most effective impact Mosaic can have on the world is to seek the transformation of Los Angeles, because it is a primary city of international influence. Mosaic expects to change the world.

The "sacred otherliness" of their mission motivates and inspires missional communities to believe the potential that can result from even a small group of believers totally committed to God's mission. They see the world as it might be if people worshipped God in every place. They know ultimate change begins in simple faith. Bishop John V. Taylor's words resonate in their hearts: "Christ's renewals and revolutions begin quietly, like faith itself. They start growing from one tiny seed, the staggering thought: *things don't have to be like this*."[2] Missional communities look at the world and at its Maker, and they know things would be much different if creation worshipped the Creator. Their desire to see people know Christ influences their actions, beginning just on the other side of their own front porch. Where they are, in their own community, is where the mission field begins.

Missions conform to spheres of influence. This means that missional responsibility begins among those with whom one has the closest relationships. It continues with intentional establishment of new relationships among those who do not know Christ. Ultimately, it extends to all the nations of the world.

Missional churches act on these principles to change the world:

- Mission begins with relationships.
- Mission is expressed in a "glocal" community.
- Missional churches identify primary mission fields.
- Missional churches touch the world.

Mission Begins with Relationships

Although church mission ministries can be expressed locally, nationally, and internationally, mission is not first about geography, but philosophy. It is not about *where* the church is, but *who* the church is, and *what it is here to accomplish*. It is not location-based but relation-based. Wherever believers are, those among whom they live and work constitute the mission field. Being missional is not first about ministering among those we do not know, but living authentically among those we do know.

If it is to be authentic, mission ministry must begin at home. As God begins to shape churches after His own heart, it is not uncommon to hear members say, "It would be easier to move and start over in a new place than to begin living missionally here." Where relationships have long existed, patterns have been established. People closest to us observe the way we live. Sometimes the statement is true that "What you're doing speaks so loudly, I can't hear what you're saying." As God begins to shape the disciple's heart, the pattern of living among those closest to us becomes paramount, because words alone will not change the assessment others make of the reality of our faith. For this reason, as disciples seek to be authentic witnesses to the transforming work of Christ in their lives, it may be helpful simply to confess to those closest to us. We might say:

> Listen, I want to ask you to forgive me. The way I have lived has not always shown the difference God is making in my life. I have been a poor witness in my words and actions. Recently, I began to realize how far I was from being the person God wanted me to be. I just wanted you to know that I am sorry for the poor example I have been as a follower of Christ. And I want to ask you to help me by pointing out when I do things you think are inappropriate for a Christian. I really want you to be able to see the difference God is making in my life. Will you forgive me and help me in this?

This apology must be genuine and specific enough to be credible. Asking others to help you by pointing out actions they deem inappropriate opens the door for dialogue about spiritual issues in Christianity. The confessor acknowledges the other as a spiritual being, asking him or her to use God-given discernment concerning morality. Importantly, it also admits the pilgrimage nature of following Christ. The process of becoming like Him is likely to include failures along the way. Of course, the apology is only effective if there is subsequent evidence of a different lifestyle. It is not easy to reclaim a spoiled reputation. It probably *would* be easier to start over somewhere else. But God has confidence in you. He has chosen to send you to the people in your immediate sphere of influence. For you, missions begins right there.

This issue has been addressed from a personal standpoint, but it has corporate application for missional congregations as well as individuals. As Fellowship Bible Church pursued God's vision in becoming a church of irresistible influence within their community, they realized the need for corporate confession. Like Israel seeking to rebuild after seventy years of Babylonian captivity, accepting ultimate responsibility for past failures resulted in brokenness and tears. They could not move ahead unless they first dealt with the past. Before Fellowship Bible Church could become salt and light in its community, confession was required. It is not always easy to become missional, beginning to live as authentic disciples, in the communities where we are well-known. But mission begins among those with whom we have the closest relationships.

Mission Is Expressed in a Glocal Community

Mission has been defined as crossing barriers with the Gospel. Today, most physical barriers that separate people have been removed. Through advancements in technology, transportation, and communications, the world has become a place of instant access. Although some countries remain closed to missionaries, virtually all countries are accessible to business and tourism. During the last fifty years, the urbanized West has seen migration among populations living near cities where better employment opportunities were found. With increased mobility suburban lifestyles developed as one could easily drive to work. Today the availability and cost efficiency of air travel and technologies have made the world one large suburb.

Recently, I had an experience that brought home to me the reality of our shrinking world. I was traveling across the United States on Amtrak

Next to me (a man from Texas) sat three college students from Seoul, Korea, who had spent the winter months working at a Colorado ski resort. Sitting behind them was a woman from Spain. She sat next to a woman from Mexico, and they chatted amiably in Spanish, despite the differences in Castilian and Mexican grammar. The Mexican woman was on the way to Canada to visit her daughter, who worked for an international banking firm. The daughter was planning on making a four-hour drive to meet her mother at the station in Seattle. But the train was running at least eight hours behind schedule, and it looked like the daughter was going to wind up waiting in the station all night for her mother. We passengers—all strangers a few hours earlier—realized that if the daughter knew the train would be late, she could complete her day's work, sleep in her own bed, and then depart for Seattle the following morning to meet the train.

But how could we reach the daughter? Coach cars do not have telephones. At this point, I happened to look at my cell phone to check the time. My phone had had no service since shortly after we left Los Angeles, but now it showed a strong signal from my own service provider. Quickly, I gave the phone to the mother from Mexico and encouraged her to call her daughter. Since she was not familiar with cell phones, her seat companion from Spain dialed the number and made the connection. Within seconds, she (the mother) was frantically telling her daughter about the new arrival time and "recommending" courses of action. Listening to the tone of this mother-daughter exchange, the young Korean woman began to laugh. Some things are evidently the same all over the world!

When the conversation was completed, the grateful mother returned the phone and asked, "May I pay you for the charges?" To which I immediately replied, "Oh, there are no charges. It was a local call!" At this, we all burst into laughter.

People from four countries, all strangers far from home, conspire together to make a cell phone call to Canada from a most beautiful but remote area of Oregon, and it is a local call! Yes, the globe is shrinking. It is in this small world that Western disciples live and work. Wherever their homes are, they have relationships with family members, friends, neighbors, and work associates. But for many, those are just a sampling of the extensive relationships they have. Although they may live in a local community, they often have relationships around the globe. Wherever those relationships are found is part of their mission field.

Today, global is local. Let's have the courage to adopt a word to describe this new state and let it stand on its own merit: *glocal*. I first heard this word used by Carol Davis, executive director of Global Spectrum ministries and missional church pioneer. She challenged churches to minister in a glocal community. Glocal is reality in the twenty-first century.

Missional Churches Identify Primary Mission Fields

Some missional congregations encourage members to identify a *primary mission field,* the sphere in which they have ongoing relationships with the largest number of unchurched people. Identification of a primary mission field assumes individual disciples are not equally responsible for sharing Christ with all persons. Greater responsibility exists among those with whom the disciple has more frequent contact and consequent opportunity for deeper personal relationships. For some, their primary mission field will be among family and extended family members; for others, their neighborhood. Many identify their workplace as the arena where they have the most relationships with pre-Christians. Some are already actively involved in an ongoing ministry or participate in a social setting through which they regularly encounter people who have no relationship with Christ. Critical factors in identifying the primary mission field are the number and depth of relationships that may be cultivated in a given setting. Ideally, it is an arena for which a disciple accepts responsibility as one sent to bear witness through words and actions to the reality of Christ's redeeming love. If no one else brings Good News to people in that environment, their access to the Gospel is still ensured.

In a typical church, members' primary mission fields might include numerous neighborhoods, schools, various businesses, a local golf course or particular sports teams, the Lions and Rotary Clubs, and the community health center staffed by church volunteers. Some fields can be defined by locations; others, such as a Little League team, are defined by affinity rather than place. As members define their primary mission fields, they become more aware of those in that environment who have not yet come to know Christ. Equipping for the missional task of apostolic evangelization becomes more relevant. Prayer for those individuals becomes an authentic missional expression as the Body gathers. Taken together, the composite primary mission field adopted by an entire church's membership can be marked on a local map. The map serves as a visual reminder of the extensive nature of the church's local mission responsibility. Further, those places in the community without any markings may point to new segments of the community in which the church might seek development of relationships.

A number of years ago, New Heights Church realized it had no relationships among school administrators or faculty. The church has concern for the development of young people and thus wanted to ensure they were able to influence the community's education processes. They decided to find a creative way to reach educators. In our interview, Matt Hannan shared the unusual strategy New Heights initiated with a public school administrator in their community:

> We made an appointment with one of the school principals. After introducing ourselves we said, "We are here on behalf of the leadership of the New Heights Church. Our folks value what you are doing in educating young people. Frankly we are here to ask you to do a favor. This is a checkbook and you will notice that the account is made out in your name. We have placed $1,000 in the account. We believe that you care for kids, and we care for kids. We want to unite on our common ground.
>
> "If we tried, we could probably find a bunch of things over which we would differ, but we don't care about those. We care that you love kids and we love kids. So we are asking you to be our agent in this school. We know you have an educational foundation available for certain needs, but we also know it can take a month to get $50 for a pair of shoes for a young person who needs them right now. Besides that, the amount you really needed was more like $75 anyway, but you were limited in the amount you could request.
>
> "So, here is a thousand dollars for you to use as needed. We are not asking you to account to us. You are a man of integrity. You will figure out some system to use in caring for the account. If you want to share that with us, that's great, but it is not required. When the amount in the checkbook is getting low, if you will let us know, we will fill it back up again. We just want to help make it a little easier for you to do what you normally do."

"When we finished talking," Hannan concluded, "there sat this big old principal, just crying like a baby."[3]

Hannan shared one result that has emerged from their strategy: "We now have eighteen members of his staff attending New Heights, and initially most of them were not Christians." New Heights finds ways to establish relationships among unreached segments of the population. They are expected to change the world, and they start from their own front porch.

Missional churches know their integrity with people in their community is fragile and important. They use various methods to determine ministry needs that may be the appropriate focus of their mission efforts. To understand the people groups within their communities, churches use demographic profiles, interviews with community agency personnel, and

MISSIONAL PRACTICE NUMBER SIX 97

community surveys to gain insight into population segments. For instance, through a *FirstView* demographic profile, a church became aware of the large percentage of single parent households with elementary-age children in their community.[4] Having no single adult members, they were unaware of their needs. Visiting with community agency leaders, including the counselor at the local elementary school, they became aware of a number of issues that are perennially present among single-parent families living in the area. After having identified the population and learning of some pressing needs, the church then investigated potential ministries they might offer to address critical needs. Using a community survey, they identified the most desired ministry that it was within their resource capacity to provide. The one they initiated, an afterschool ministry for latchkey children, has become a model in the community. Over time, the face of the congregation changed to include a significant number of single parents.

In their own communities, churches are finding new ways to establish caring relationships with people who are not yet on the journey to knowing God. But their concern is also resulting in mission ministries throughout the nation and in other countries.

Missional Churches Touch the World

Missional congregations communicate God's activity in the world, just as they teach God's word. Their passion for the nations can often be seen the moment one enters the church's facility. At NorthWood Church for the Communities, an entire wall of the foyer is a world map featuring pull-out information and photographs from nations where the church is involved in missions. The prayer room of Antioch Community Church provides information concerning those nations where Antioch members are starting churches. Antioch has also developed Antioch Ministries International (AMI) to facilitate sending church planters throughout the earth. AMI missionaries raise their own financial support. By 2002, AMI had established churches in three continents and had church planters in twenty-two countries.

In a global community, either missional churches are involved in glocal missions or they are extraneous. Erwin McManus could not imagine Mosaic *not* having hands-on concern and involvement in the nations of the world. He said in our interview, "For Mosaic, a primary focus has been sending people around the world. About 150 of our congregation have left for the 10/40 Window [that area of North Africa, the Middle East, and Asia between latitudes 10° and 40° north of the equator containing the most 'unreached' people groups with desperate physical needs] during the last ten years. From new-member orientation on, we talk about 'taking on the planet.' We have members from about fifty different nations. If we were not talking and acting on a global level, they would say we were irrelevant. Our people's best friends are living around the world. So it is natural for our people to be there also."

Many missional churches develop ongoing relationships with particular countries. They often begin through a single relationship. One church assists house churches that are being planted in a "closed" country. The church's connection with the country began when one church family hosted an international exchange student in their home. During the year together, the student and the family's daughter became "sisters." Like good sisters, they shared everything, including faith. When the girl returned to her country, it was natural for the American host family to go visit their "adopted daughter" and meet her family. Now, some years later, the seeds of faith sown through those relationships continue to bear fruit. Trips back and forth continue among additional families as their relationships deepen.

One person whose position title is minister of missions shared the emotional experience that influenced his church to continue ministering in the same nation year after year. "When we carried the first mission team, we met a young girl who, as is often the case, spoke some English. One of our members asked her if she knew Jesus. She paused thoughtfully for a moment, repeated the name 'Jesus,' and replied, 'No, he not from around here.'" Today her face and words, imprinted in the corporate memory of the church, continue to motivate their commitment to missions.

In various ways, missional congregations are making a difference in the world. In countries where devastating disasters have occurred, churches develop NGOs (nongovernmental organizations) to provide compassionate relief and development in the name of Christ. In the aftermath of wars, churches are learning how to partner effectively with governmental agencies in nation building. Through servant evangelism, they are touching lives and sharing the love of God with people from across the tracks and around the world. They are involved in glocal missions. Theirs is a hands-on mission involvement.

Although missional churches expect to change the world from their own front porch (a colloquial expression used to indicate their involvement beginning locally and extending globally), the missional passion that all the nations might worship God must outpace the capacity for local church involvement. Giving only toward that in which our congregation can be directly involved is the epitome of selfishness. Such practice stands in opposition to the missional passion expressed in the heart of God, who led John to record, "You will do well to send them on their way in a manner worthy of God. For they went out for the sake of the Name. . . . Therefore, we ought to support such men, that we may be fellow-workers with the truth" (3 John 6–8). Missional churches are such fellow workers, partners in the Gospel, sometimes directly involved, sometimes supporting others whom God sends. Their passion is God's passion for the nations, and through the Gospel they expect to change the world.

Reflection and Application

1. Reflect on God's transformation of your life. How are the lives of your friends being transformed by Him?

2. Contrast your church's global experience of one decade past with today. What evidence and responses do you observe related to the shrinking globe?

3. If people in your community were to say "What you're doing speaks so loudly, I can't hear what you're saying!" what priorities would they attribute to your church on the basis of their observing your actions?

4. Have new ministry initiatives begun with the intent to reach previously unreached segments of your area population? Propose actions to affirm those responsible for and involved in new ministries.

SUGGESTED READING

Johnstone, P., and Mandryk, J. *Operation World: When We Pray God Works.* Waynesboro, Ga.: Paternoster USA, 2001.

Lane, P. *A Beginner's Guide to Crossing Cultures: Making Friends in a Multicultural World.* Downer's Grove, Ill.: InterVarsity Press, 2002.

Silvoso, E. *Anointed for Business: How Christians Can Use Their Influence in the Marketplace to Change the World.* Ventura, Calif.: Regal Press, 2002.

Missional Practice Assessment

Rate each statement that follows from 1 (the statement is not true of our church) to 7 (the statement is true of our church) by circling the appropriate response. The greatest insight will be gained if you avoid selecting 4 as a response. Please use that selection minimally. When you are finished, transfer your responses to the assessments in the Appendix and total your scores to find your net response. Your group's response to these assessments gives a clear picture of your church's readiness to move to being missional.

Members believe our church is making a major difference in the world.

1   2   3   4   5   6   7

Our church has a vital prayer ministry focusing on updated mission concerns.

1   2   3   4   5   6   7

Most members have identified their primary mission field.

1   2   3   4   5   6   7

Our church has strategies for reaching new people groups in our area.

1   2   3   4   5   6   7

Our members intentionally cultivate global relationships.

1   2   3   4   5   6   7

Our worship regularly emphasizes the member's missionary involvement.

1   2   3   4   5   6   7

Most of our members participate in short-term mission projects.

1   2   3   4   5   6   7

9

MISSIONAL PRACTICE NUMBER SEVEN

ORDER ACTIONS ACCORDING TO PURPOSE

---

*But Jesus said to him, "No one, having put his hand to the plow,
and looking back, is fit for the kingdom of God."*

—Luke 9:62

*Depend upon it—God's work done in
God's way will never lack supplies.*

—J. Hudson Taylor

MISSIONAL CHURCHES do what they do for specific reasons. They are
clear about their task, and they have accepted responsibility for accomplishing that task. Not willing to be dissuaded by those with other opinions nor diverted by other courses of action, they order their actions
according to their purpose.

Rick Warren, pastor of Saddleback Community Church, has written
two immensely popular books, *The Purpose Driven Church* and *The Purpose Driven Life*. The premise of both books underscores the importance
of activities being congruent with an overarching purpose. Whether in the

life of an individual or in a church, achievement of purpose is realized only when the activities to which one commits time and resources are purposeful. Warren says, "There are many 'good' things you can do with your life, but God's purposes are . . . essentials you *must* do. Unfortunately, it's easy to get distracted and forget what is most important. It's easy to drift away from what matters most and slowly get off course."[1]

Ordering actions on the basis of purpose means missional churches possess clarity of purpose. They regularly analyze their practices against their purpose. Although it is difficult, they stop doing things that are not helpful in achieving their purpose. They also require their practices to be culturally relevant, scripturally sound, and congruent with their purpose.

Missional communities use purpose to guide their actions in these ways:

- They know their purpose.
- They check that actions are based upon purpose.
- They let go of what does not serve their purpose.
- They do only what serves their purpose.

They Know Their Purpose

Some might say all churches have the same purpose, according to the New Testament accounts of the Great Commandment and Great Commission. But purpose is more than simply a statement of mission; it is a local expression identifying the part of that universal mission an individual church senses as its responsibility. It is the composite of a church's ongoing activities facilitated by underlying values. In this regard, there is a strong corollary between a church's culture and its purpose. The purpose is the strategic goal of an organization. The culture is the environment in which that strategic goal is pursued. If the culture does not embrace values that can result in accomplishing the strategic goal, either the culture must be changed (a uniquely challenging prospect) or the purpose must be restated. It is easier to change a purpose statement than to change culture to an environment in which a new purpose can be accomplished.

Missional churches are clear about their purpose. The purpose of Christ Episcopal Church in Overland Park, Kansas, is "making disciples who make disciples for Jesus Christ." This statement is the framework for all church activities. Similarly, although Grace Point Church exists "to lead unsaved people to a relationship of full devotion to Jesus Christ," the framework is further expressed in the "G5 characteristics" of a fully devoted follower of Christ: grace, growth, gifts, give, go. Each of those characteristics is thoroughly explained, enabling members to express the church's purpose more precisely and practically. In fulfillment of its purpose, "a passion for Jesus and for His purposes in the earth," Antioch Community Church has five "strategic goals" they are laboring to implement:

1. Lead people to Jesus daily.
2. Equip people to use their gifts.
3. Pursue and practice the presence of God.
4. Plant reproducing churches.
5. Facilitate becoming a multicultural congregation.

The mission statement of Mosaic is "to live by faith, to be known by love, and to be a voice of hope," but a more extensive statement of their purpose is "to be a spiritual reference point throughout Los Angeles and a sending base to the ends of the earth."

In each instance, the congregation has drawn a word picture of what fulfillment of their purpose would look like. They know their purpose. Frequently the purpose statement is prominently displayed in church publications and properties, and it is etched into the memory of its members. The purpose of a mission statement is not simply to be posted or memorized, but to activate people to do things that yield accomplishment of the strategic goal. The additional statements furnished in support of each of these mission or purpose statements allow the churches to make their mission statements actionable.

Corporate management expert Peter Drucker writes about purpose statements: "A mission statement has to be operational, otherwise it's just good intentions. A mission statement has to focus on what the institution really tries to do and then do it so that everybody in the organization can say, 'This is *my* contribution to the goal.'"[2] Through additional explanations, each of the missional communities identified here has made its mission statement operational. That is, they all have a clearly stated purpose that can inform strategic goals.

They Check That Actions Are Based upon Purpose

Strategy is allocation of current resources to tomorrow's purpose. Action is incremental performance in fulfillment of strategy. Performance, what is done moment by moment, will result in fulfillment of strategies and ultimate accomplishment of a stated purpose, will evidence that the strategies were not appropriate to the stated purpose, or will reveal that the stated purpose was not the actual purpose. Anytime performance does not enhance accomplishment of the *stated* purpose, then the performance *is* the *actual* purpose. More than what is stated, what is done reveals purpose. Actions speak louder than words. To accomplish purpose, missional churches analyze their current practices against their ultimate purpose. They check that actions are based upon purpose.

The real purpose of a church may be assessed through a number of diagnostic indicators: the calendar of activities, participation record, budget expenditures, and so on. To check that actions are based upon purpose, one might review the activities included in the church's schedule of events. Typically, they include corporate worship times, Bible study classes, weekday ministries designed primarily for either members of the church or people in the community, some specific outreach evangelism activity, discipleship life-skill training, and choral or drama rehearsals. For every activity, it is appropriate to ask: "How does this activity or event lead to the accomplishment of our purpose or mission?" "Is this activity designed for members or to connect with those who are not yet members?" "If we were not already doing this activity, would we initiate it today, on the basis of our mission and purpose?"

At Mosaic, determination concerning new ministries or events is made from a simple process of evaluation. Erwin McManus states: "We do everything and anything that emerges out of our core values. If it affirms the five core values, we do it. If it doesn't, we do not do it. And there are all kinds of things we do *not* do."[3]

A second but significant part of the assessment should include the participation level in events. This is significant because a schedule of events does not indicate how many people are involved. Simply because an event is on the calendar does not mean that it is a priority within the church. Among some evangelical groups it is typical to find "prayer meeting" listed, perhaps on Wednesday evenings. One might think its inclusion would indicate a priority placed on prayer in the life of the church. However, when reviewing the participation level in this event, one might find only a small percentage of members attending. Further, the title given to the event might be misleading; one could find "prayer meeting" to be a brief service including congregational singing, shared updates on the physical condition of ill or aging members, a devotional or Bible lesson, and only a short time of actual prayer. Neither its inclusion in the calendar nor the name used to describe it point to the real purpose of the time, or to the value it holds for the membership.

To determine actual purpose and mission, one needs to investigate the actual nature and participation level of events listed in the schedule of activities. It is actual performance, what the members really participate in, that evidences real value.

A second diagnostic indicator of purpose is the record of expenditures—the budget. How a church spends its financial resources reflects the priorities and the understanding of the nature of church. Bob Roberts described NorthWood Church for the Community's process for determining budget allocations: "We listen for what God wants us to do, and then we dedicate the resources required to do it." In our interview, he further identified one of the greatest threats faced as "not allowing the abundant blessing of financial resources to dilute our focus on doing what God has instructed us to do." There are always people willing to advance their own agenda concerning how finances should be used. The tension is to ensure funds are allocated to fulfill purpose.

Traditional church budgets usually have a significant portion of total expenditures dedicated to staff compensation, property debt reduction, utilities, operating expenses, and maintenance. A lesser amount is usually allocated to ongoing ministry programs designed primarily for members. Generally, smaller allocations facilitate evangelism and mission ministry in the local church setting and beyond.

A number of churches are developing patterns unlike the traditional model, including cell and house churches. Sometimes called "simple churches," these communities typically do not invest a large percentage of their financial resources in purchasing facilities. As a result, simple church missional communities reflect a much higher percentage of their total expenditures to caring ministries within the local community and to missions beyond the locale. Although they may not be considered by some as a "real church" (sadly implying real churches must have buildings and operate in a more traditional model), simple churches should be commended for the disproportionate amount of missional costs they underwrite through their mission gifts. It is not unusual for a simple church to dedicate as much as 80 percent of its total offerings to mission purposes beyond the local community. In fact, these churches seek to invert the traditional church percentages, where typically only 15–20 percent of resources are allocated to mission causes beyond the local church.

Without regard to the type of congregation, traditional or simple, the manner in which financial resources are invested is an indicator of purpose and priority of a church. No matter what the purpose statement may say, practical distribution of resources is an authentic statement of the real purpose of a congregation. If the stated purpose and allocated resources continue at odds over the long run, one can rightly dismiss the stated purpose as rhetoric. Performance is the purpose.

They Let Go of What Does Not Serve Their Purpose

A third implication in ordering actions according to purpose involves the acuity with which congregations cease activities not contributing to their purpose. Churches tend to be much better at initiating new activities than they are at discontinuing old ones. Once a church has begun a practice, it quickly becomes part of "the way we do things here." Discontinuance of activities is generally accompanied by outcry from a small contingent who benefit from, enjoy participating in, or otherwise believe the activity should be continued. Often more emotional than rational, those lobbying for continuation of programs or events may expend great energy in persuading the congregation of their perceived significance. Often churches find it easier to continue the activity than to deal with conflict. Letting go is not easy.

The challenge of discontinuing practices is not unique to churches. Addressing change, Drucker identifies policies that must be implemented if any business is to successfully manage change. Foundational to all other policies is one he calls "organized abandonment," which consists of "abandoning yesterday"—freeing up resources committed to things that may have worked in the past but are not working today.[4]

Traditional churches seeking to become missional communities find ways to celebrate the successes of the past without requiring the continuance of ministry initiatives that were effective then. Many Western churches look back to another era as their most successful period of growth and ministry. When church members see their church's best days as lying in the past, rather than believing they lie in the future, the events of yesterday's calendar come to hold magical power. Many struggling congregations seek to go back to the future, instead of valuing yesterday's experience as they faithfully walk toward tomorrow.

Antioch Community Church does not continue activities that cannot be sustained by its values. As Jimmy Seibert acknowledged, "We are learning to love God in a real life-giving way. We are learning to love each other in ways that build life-giving relationships. We are trying to reach people who are hurting, who don't know about Christ, but who are interested in knowing Him. It is nothing fancy," he concluded, "but we are wholeheartedly committed to those three things. Anything in our ministries or in our programs that serves those ends, we will do. If it does not serve those ends, we will not do it, whether at the individual, the cell or the corporate expression. Our value base drives everything."[5]

Measuring every event and activity according to its contribution to the church's purpose is not easy—in fact, it can be painful. But no organization can continue to invest in new directions without discontinuing others.

To do so would rob all activities of the potential for excellence. No church can do everything. Each must identify those ministries that it should do, and do them with excellence. Fractured focus results in mediocrity.

Some churches try to do too many things, while other churches do too many things of the *same type*, a phenomenon often observed by consultants who assist churches in strategic planning. Most churches identify the traditional functions of the church as worship, education, witness, ministry, and fellowship. Although other words may be used in designating them (for instance, evangelism instead of witness), these are generally accepted as the five primary functions around which activities of churches develop. When seeking to weigh actions against a church's purpose, members have a unique ability to judge every activity as filling one of these functions, and they therefore assume these activities all contribute toward accomplishment of the church's purpose. However, no attention may have been given to the balance of emphases.

Consumer or maintenance-minded churches tend to design most of their events for members. Missional churches exist to reach those who are not yet part of the church, and so design activities that connect them with people outside the church. Churches without a missional focus can assess their activities according to their purpose and find no need to change or discontinue any events. Continuing status quo is completely acceptable, for these churches, even if the result of continuing those actions would not contribute to accomplishing the commission Christ gave His church.

Churches need to develop caring relationships among believers. Fellowship is critical. However, a church that fashions all of its activities toward enhanced fellowship among members cannot claim it exists for the purpose of reaching lost people. It exists to develop strong social relationships among its members. Again, performance *is* purpose. Where classic functions of the church are used to define purpose, careful attention must be given to a balanced distribution among *all* the functions with regard to events calendared.

When missional churches order their actions according to their purpose, they must continuously let go of those activities that do not result in accomplishing their purpose. They must be ruthless in this difficult endeavor. As Drucker puts it, "The question has to be asked . . . 'If we did not do this already, would we, knowing what we now know, go into it?'" If the answer is no, he says, we must decide on new courses of action.[6] Some find it easier to say, "Let's make another study" or "What we are doing is meaningful to some people" than to say, "It is a good thing, but it is not helping us achieve our primary purpose. Let it go!" It is only the latter response that orders actions according to purpose.

They Do Only What Serves Their Purpose

It is important to know your purpose, check your actions against that purpose, and stop doing activities that do not further your purpose. But it is critical to do those things that result in accomplishing your purpose. All the analysis possible does not result in pursuit of purpose without action.

Seemingly every denomination has inserted its own title into this often-repeated adaptation of the familiar nursery rhyme:

> Mary had a little lamb,
> it could have been a sheep;
> it joined the local [fill in your own] church,
> and died from lack of sleep!

Missional churches know members have many demands on their time, so the events they offer are strategic and excellent. They do not confuse activity with accomplishment.

The quantity of activities calendared is not a measure of purposeful effectiveness. Missional communities seek to be strategic as they calendar events. They realize the best "new opportunity" considered, if it does not further the purpose of the church, is not an opportunity at all. It is a diversion. It would divert time, resources, and energy *from* the purpose rather than toward it. For those who order actions according to purpose, this is not acceptable.

Churches must determine the appropriate response to a constant barrage of opportunities. In Los Angeles, seeking to be a church for the unchurched, Mosaic has repeatedly faced challenges to incorporate activities or practices of other churches into their experience. As disciples from other churches relocate to Los Angeles and visit Mosaic, they often find its energy and dynamism refreshing. Not infrequently, leaders at Mosaic hear people say, "If you could just include a traditional hymn or two in your services, our family would feel comfortable becoming members of Mosaic." In response, they tell the newcomer:

> We are honored that you would consider becoming part of the Mosaic family. We have made an intentional choice about the music we include in worship. While traditional hymns are meaningful to many who have long been part of the church, their imagery is often unclear to those never exposed to the Gospel. We are determined to be a church for those persons. That is why we do what we do. That is our purpose. There must be a thousand churches in LA that sing hymns. We know many of them as caring communities of faith. If traditional hymns are important to you, let us help you find one of those churches.[7]

Sometimes, the prospective members find other churches with which to unite. But Mosaic knows they cannot fulfill the desire of every individual. They serve an audience of One and seek to fulfill His purpose through their actions.

Maintaining a singular focus is vital to accomplishing purpose. Jimmy Seibert accepts few invitations to share the Antioch Community story, explaining: "I say 'No' to about 90 percent of speaking engagements and opportunities, not because I am not honored nor because I do not want to serve others, but because we have not yet become what we want to become. *It takes everything you have in life, 100 percent of your life, to see one of these churches come to pass.*"[8] There are many good things disciples and their churches could do. Those who intend to be missional know they cannot be everything and do everything. They are focused on the purpose for which they have been sent and they are not taking their eyes off of that purpose. They order their actions according to their purpose.

Reflection and Application

1. Review your church's calendar of activities. For each item, indicate which of the five functions of the church each event is designed to accomplish. Throughout the process, make a count of the number of times each function is listed. Once completed, discover and discuss implications of this exercise with other church leaders.

2. Devise a plan for asking 20 percent of active church members to state the purpose of your church. Record all answers as they are given. Assess the uniformity or discontinuity of those responses. Does your church have a statement of purpose? In what ways is it actionable?

3. Reflect on this statement from Peter Drucker: "The change leader puts every product, every service, every process, every market, every distribution channel, every customer and end-use, on trial for its life. And it does so on a regular schedule. The question has to be asked—and asked seriously—'If we did not do this already, would we, knowing what we now know, go into it?'" If you introduced this philosophy to your church's calendaring process, what differences might result?

Suggested Reading

Warren, R. *The Purpose Driven Church: Growth Without Compromising Your Message and Mission.* Grand Rapids, Mich.: Zondervan, 1995.

Missional Practice Assessment

Rate each statement that follows from 1 (the statement is not true of our church) to 7 (the statement is true of our church) by circling the appropriate response. The greatest insight will be gained if you avoid selecting 4 as a response. Please use that selection minimally. When you are finished, transfer your responses to the assessments in the Appendix and total your scores to find your net response. Your group's response to these assessments gives a clear picture of your church's readiness to move to being missional.

Members are very clear about our church's purpose.

1   2   3   4   5   6   7

We calendar only events that help us accomplish our purpose.

1   2   3   4   5   6   7

Our programs are flexible, leaving room for God to direct changes.

1   2   3   4   5   6   7

We are good at celebrating the starting *and* closing of ministries.

1   2   3   4   5   6   7

Items in our budget reflect our missional priorities.

1   2   3   4   5   6   7

Our programs and ministries give evidence of our commitment to excellence.

1   2   3   4   5   6   7

We would rather lose a prospect than violate our purpose.

1   2   3   4   5   6   7

10

MISSIONAL PRACTICE NUMBER EIGHT

MEASURE GROWTH BY CAPACITY
TO RELEASE, NOT RETAIN

---

*Most assuredly, I say to you, unless a grain of
wheat falls into the ground and dies, it remains alone;
but if it dies, it produces much grain.*

—John 12:24

*One lesson some of us have come to learn is this, that in
divine service the principle of waste is the principle of power.
The principle which determines usefulness is the very principle
of scattering. Real usefulness in the hand of God is measured in
terms of "waste." The principle of waste is the principle that He
would have govern us. . . . True satisfaction is brought to the heart
of God when we are really, as people would think, "wasting"
ourselves upon him. It seems as though we are giving too much
and getting nothing—and that is the secret of pleasing God.*

—Watchman Nee, from *The Normal Christian Life*

"FROM THE MOMENT new members come in, we are preparing them to go back out." This statement was made about Christ Fellowship Church, but it could be perhaps the most distinctive missional axiom: missional churches measure growth by their capacity to release rather than retain. When I asked missional members about the growth of their church during the last year, one responded, "There was a section of our community we were not effectively reaching. We started a new ministry there and are now seeing people come to Christ." Another said, "There was no church in a town near us, so we gave six families to go and start a church there."

Such statements are a natural response when asked of growth in missional churches. They think first of extension, not enlargement; of releasing members in the power of God's Spirit, not in retaining them. Clearly, these churches define growth differently from most traditional churches, which usually consider releasing members as loss rather than growth. But in missional communities, the ultimate objective is every member released to serve in God's mission. These churches equip members to be sent out. They empower and release members to community ministries, begin new cells, or start new churches. In each instance, these congregations understand that releasing results in growth.

Most of us associate growth with success, but success can be defined in various ways. Maintenance churches generally regard success as an increase in the number of active members or the construction of additional facilities. Some have identified the three B's as classic measurements of growth: buildings, budgets, and baptisms. In this business mentality environment, a ministry that does not result in added numbers, additional revenue, or increased recognition of the church has little prospect for long-term continuation. Ultimately, if it is not bringing new people into the church, it is not a success.

For missional churches, the goal of church growth is not to get bigger. The goal is to equip more people to live as authentic disciples of Jesus Christ. The measure has to do with function, not size. Enlargement is a by-product rather than the focus of growth in missional churches. In our bigger-is-better world, where Mom and Pop shops are lost to big-box discount stores, small has been associated with unsuccessful. But we still hunger for the intimacy of a small restaurant where every dish is prepared with detailed authenticity. We still choose the small auto repair shop where we trust the mechanic's skill and honesty. The measure of success is ultimately not about size, but about service.

When the focus is on serving and sending rather than numerical growth, this is what we see reflected in faith communities:

- They grow naturally.
- They connect with a source of unlimited supply.
- They see themselves as the mission-sending agency of God's design.
- They take a role in equipping missional leaders.
- They see multiplication as God's design for reaching new generations.

They Grow Naturally

God's instruction to "be fruitful and multiply" has historically required little encouragement. It's a natural growth process: families have children. Their children grow and have children. The result, within just three to four generations, is exponential; multiplication rather than addition grows the human family. This is also the New Testament method for developing new disciples. Retrieving a King James term, Bill Tinsley, a practitioner and student of church planting, somewhat humorously referred to this natural phenomenon as the "begetting process." "To multiply," he said, "churches must use the age-old process of begetting. It is one of the most powerful forces at work in the world."[1]

If the church exists to equip more people to become authentic disciples of Jesus Christ, there must be caring communities into which those disciples can be born and grow. God's design for procreation is multiplying family units: "For this reason a man shall leave his father and his mother, and be joined to his wife, and they shall become one flesh" (Genesis 2:24). Children are born into new family units, and parents release their children to begin their own families.

In the same way, if an exponential number of new disciples are to be born and equipped, churches "planning for multiplied disciples must plan for multiplied churches."[2] Just as families release their children when they have grown to maturity, churches release disciples as they are equipped for their missionary role. The willingness of missional churches to release members indicates those churches have come to appreciate their connection with a source of unlimited supply, their identity as the mission-sending agency of God's design, their role in equipping missional leaders, and multiplication as God's design for reaching new generations.

They Connect with a Source of Unlimited Supply

We can also describe the natural releasing and multiplying design embraced by missional churches as "biotic." According to Christian Schwarz, ecologists define biotic potential as "inherent capacity of an organism or species to reproduce and survive."[3] As churches release members to ministry and mission, they tap into their biotic potential and find an unlimited supply of dynamic energy. In Scripture, this source is referred to as springs of living water (John 4:14). In the Old Testament, God attributed to His people this evil: "They have forsaken Me, the fountain of living waters, to hew for themselves cisterns, broken cisterns that can hold no water" (Jeremiah 2:13). Where there was an uncontained and unlimited supply, God's people elected instead broken containers unable to hold any water. Missional churches have established connection with the source of unlimited supply, a biotic potential similar to an artesian well.

In Arkansas there is a bottling plant at the source of an underground spring. Visitors can see the process used to pump the spring water to the surface and ultimately into various bottles used in its distribution. The plant consumes extensive amounts of energy in extracting spring water from deep within the earth. Along a roadside near Athens, Texas, is an artesian well. Residents come from miles around to fill containers with the pure artesian water that flows in unending supply from its source. Both sources produce water. The former requires energy to extract, while the latter would require energy to restrict the flow. The artesian well requires no pump; its flow to the surface is a natural phenomenon. It continues day and night, year after year. It is uncontrolled, natural.

The artesian well parallels the image of dynamic energy available as churches release members into God's mission. Not only do missional churches tap into the unlimited supply of God's energy source, they produce energy. According to Brian McLaren, a church is "a self-sustaining organization that does ministry and produces a surplus of energy and money over time. In other words, it attends to its own needs and, in so doing, miraculously generates more than it needs, so it can give to needs beyond its own borders."[4] With every member released, community ministry begun, and every new church started, the first law of thermodynamics is broken. New energy is created.

Releasing members has more to do with the mentality than the locality associated with their sending. Craig Van Gelder, professor of congregational mission at Luther Seminary in St. Paul, Minnesota, and author of *The Essence of the Church*, identifies two Scriptural expressions into which members are released: "local missional congregations and mobile missional teams who in turn plant new missional congregations."[5] Some stay while others go, but all are released to serve. In that releasing, the principle of multiplication produces astounding results. Schwarz confirms the principle's potential when he describes the world's largest church, in Seoul, Korea, which has 750,000 members. The church, he says, grew this large "only because the principle of multiplication was carefully observed from the beginning. . . . It really consists of a network of sub-congregations that originated through multiplication. These sub-congregations are then built on a network of continuously multiplying small groups."[6]

Whether released to serve in a missional church ministry, or as part of a mobile missional team starting a new church, the release of members is divinely energized by the artesian well of God's Spirit. Through its connection with that power source, the church is God's authentic sending agency.

They See Themselves as the Mission-Sending Agency of God's Design

In the Early Church, the local church was the agent of God's sending. But with the development of the modern missionary movement, responsibility for sending missionaries transferred to missionary societies and denominational boards. Ultimately, church members came to assume that missionaries are professionally trained persons selected and sent by specialized agencies with acumen in developing specific strategies for various national contexts.

Writing in the 1920s, Roland Allen, an Anglican missionary in China from 1895 to 1903, described two organizations for missionary work. One, the organization of missionary societies, he called "cumbrous." The other he identified as simple: the Church. In his estimation, it is "established and organized with a world-wide mission for a world-wide work . . . a living organism composed of living souls deriving their life from Christ, who was its Head. . . . It was the organization of a missionary body."[7]

Allen's missionary experience pointed him toward a critical flaw in missionary patterns developed in Christendom. His assessment of the state of the church remains true today. In large measure the church has forgotten its original character, its essence. In the words of Carol Davis, "The church in America has amnesia and needs to recover its memory"[8] of God's story, a love story of His longing for all the nations to worship Him. Churches also need to reclaim memory of being His people. Every believer has the privilege of being His missionary to their world. The church must also reclaim the memory of God's purpose, to disciple the nations. The West has been abundantly blessed with churches and freedoms, but it has failed to display holiness among the nations. Some view the moral standards of the West as among the poorest in the world. Rather than being a discipler of the nations, the Western church has often abdicated responsibility to its representative missionary agencies. No other organization can fulfill the task God gave to the organism of His design, the church.

Today, missional churches are reclaiming their role as the agent through which God sends His missionary people. At Grace Point Church members are assisted to identify their spiritual gifts and find ministries through which they can regularly express their missionary role together with other members of the Body. Every member is part of a servant group, a place where the community lives out its gifts and passion. One of Grace Point's core values is "ownership (take it!) . . . responsibly creating and carrying out meaningful ministry in an excellent way." Likewise, NorthWood Church prepares members for the missionary role and includes a commitment to serve as part of the membership covenant.

At the core of the Fellowship Bible Church's commitment to be a church of irresistible influence is the deployment of all adult members into places of ministry in which they can capably serve and about which they can be passionate. For three years, following newcomer orientation, believers are equipped in Seasons of Life groups. These life-stage–specific groups assist believers in developing community with fellow believers, deepening their spiritual life and prepare them to move into their ministry role in a Common Cause service group. No one is allowed to stay indefinitely in an equipping mode without an ultimate place of personal ministry. Everyone who joins Fellowship Bible Church knows he or she will be sent to serve. Fellowship has broadened its concept of ministry to include members' service as volunteers in community agencies, schools, and other human service providers. They are making a difference well beyond the confines of Fellowship Bible Church.

Most churches might begin their mission focus at home and subsequently extend to the nations, but Antioch Community Church's global sending process grew as a result of Jimmy Seibert's observation. "Back in 1987," he explained, "two great influences were Youth with a Mission and Campus Crusade. They didn't just offer [students] a good experience in college, they offered them the world. That was the impetus for our asking, 'Can the church own the training and sending process?'

"The church was not offering them the world through their relationships and development inside the local church," he asserted. Therefore students would go to a parachurch organization, seminary, or another agency because they did not feel they could fulfill the destiny of God out of their church.

"So," Seibert continued, "what I said was, 'We are going to start at the "st" of "uttermost" and work our way back.' And that is what we have done. We started out in southern Siberia and Mongolia and today we are in some of the most challenging places in the world. We have sent out ten new church plants since we started the church three years ago. All except one have been overseas. . . . Literally, we have hundreds, if not more than a thousand, per year who go out on short-term missions."[9]

At the same time that Antioch is releasing members to start churches, they continue to add new members and experience numerical growth locally. More than seventeen hundred people attend; the Antioch membership has grown to more than twelve hundred persons. The membership comprises roughly 60 percent young career families and 35 percent college students. An area of new growth is among older adults who are hungry to invest the rest of their lives in a church that is touching the world for Christ.

It's not only larger congregations that can be missional. Missional churches come in all sizes. Iglesia Hosanna, a rural church in an area of Texas near the Mexican border, called pastor Juan Flores four years ago. The church averaged about thirty-five people in worship services. One Sunday morning Flores shared a concern with his congregation. "There is a community about seventeen miles down the road that does not have a church. We need to ask God to impress upon a couple of our families to go there and start a church. We will train one of you to be the pastor."

As one might guess, the reaction of the congregation was dubious. "Pastor, we cannot afford to give away two families. We are too small." But they did, and about a year later, Iglesia Hosanna was averaging about sixty-five people in worship. Again, the pastor challenged the church to give families to start a new church in another community. This time the reaction of the congregation was moderated, "Do you think we can?" Again, they did. Pastor Flores's face beams as he tells the story of what happened about a year later when the church had grown to 105 people in worship. He was approached by a deacon one Sunday morning who said, "Pastor, some of us have been talking. There is a community about twenty-five miles from here without a church. We believe it is time for us to send some families over there to start a new church." No longer dubious, releasing members to start churches is now in the missional DNA of Iglesia Hosanna.

They Take a Role in Equipping Missional Leaders

What about the people who are released? Can they really be replaced? Inevitably, well-intentioned optimists will say, "God always replaces that which we give away to Him," or "We can never out-give God." Erwin McManus says that such statements "make nice greeting cards, but they are not always precisely true. Sometimes when you release a 'ten-talent' leader, God gives you in her place ten 'one-talent' people. The training and equipping process has to run its course before they can begin to replace the service provided by the ten-talent leader." Clearly, as the church reclaims its identity as the sending agency of God's design, it must also enhance commitment to its role in equipping missional leaders.

Leadership development is perhaps the greatest challenge missional churches face. The lack of leaders possessing an apostolic orientation severely limits the rapid expansion of the church. In North America, professional academic preparation is the accepted route for church leaders. Those who sense God's sending into mission vocations are encouraged first to complete an undergraduate degree and then to pursue three or four years of postgraduate education at a seminary. Seminary education encourages theoretical and analytical observation in classroom settings distanced from actual ministry environments.

Because the model is classroom-oriented, students must live on or near a seminary campus so that they can attend classes regularly. Their isolation from actual ministry settings results in a theoretical instructional format rather than a pragmatic process in which learning can be applied and assessed in practice. Students who have spent years in the challenging environment of academia often find it difficult to relate in the cultures from which they came or to which they sensed God's sending. During their educational experience they have become different people, acquiring new tastes and enjoying the accoutrements of the academic system.

Alan Roxburgh considers the need for models that can equip missional leaders for the church exiled in a changing culture. "Exile," he writes, "requires more than the priest, pedagogue, or professional."[10] If seminaries are to be relevant in training missional leaders in the future, drastic changes will be required. They must move from a theoretical education, accomplished in separation from the mission field, to a practical applied education obtained in the context of mission ministry.

Just as the church must reclaim its role as the primary sending agency, it must also own the task of Christian education. Other entities, universities, and seminaries assist the church in that task, but it is hard to find Scriptural foundation for requiring professional training of ministers. Certainly the early fishermen apostles possessed no academic credentials in ministry. Of them it was said, "Now as they observed the confidence of Peter and John and understood that they were uneducated and untrained men, they were amazed, and began to recognize them as having been with Jesus" (Acts 4:13). Notice, however, the text identifies the lack of formal education neither as a limitation nor an advantage. Observers recognized the leadership acumen possessed by the apostles and attributed it to an alternative form of education: they had "been with Jesus." Today, missional churches are again providing alternative education for a new generation of apostolic leaders. Some minister in their local area. Others carry the Gospel into the neighborhoods where they live. In some instances, they are trained as new church planters. All are equipped to be missionaries wherever they live, work, or play. Churches are the primary equipping center for apostolic missional leaders.

Some churches are joining with seminaries or other academic institutions to offer intern programs through which students wed theory to practice in the laboratory of the church. Often fashioned around the core concern of church planting, churches like NorthWood Church for the Communities provide interns the opportunity to learn while doing. Interns observe senior church planters and learn from their actions. Ultimately, they begin a church plant with the guidance and support of those church planters under whose auspices they studied. Students gain both church-starting experience and academic credit as they participate in the internship.

New Heights Church continued to have requests from potential church planters who wanted the opportunity to spend time at New Heights and learn their processes. In response, New Heights initiated Northwest Church Planting as their church-planter training arm. New Heights provides the laboratory in which interns learn; Northwest Church Planting was developed as a separate not-for-profit entity. By creating a distinct and separate organization in which to train church planters, New Heights was able to extend invitations to church planters affiliated with other churches, who would not have felt comfortable sending their church planters to another church for training. Through Northwest Church Planting, New Heights has provided training and support for church plants around the world and among various evangelical denominations.

These examples are designed to furnish training for those who are not members of the sponsoring churches. Antioch Community Church has developed a training center whose primary focus is equipping its members for church planting. This nonaccredited process includes both an intensive eight-month track and an extended eleven-month evening track. Jimmy Seibert says that Antioch's method of preparing members to be sent out as church planters begins with the cell system: "Members have relationships in small group communities where they are being discipled, discipling others, and sharing Christ. We have observed this is an excellent initial process for developing people as church planters. It's the old adage, 'If you don't do it here then you won't do it there.' Only those who have been in cell leadership are accepted into our training school [which] provides more in-depth focus in some of the traditional courses such as the life and teachings of Christ, Old and New Testament surveys, cross-cultural ministry, church-planting development, and issues dealing with personal character development."[11]

During this time students are evaluated by Antioch's church planting office, which assesses their personal history and personal life. If they are then accepted as a full-time church planter, they go through two weeks of values training. "This is an in-depth revisitation of our core values," Seibert says. "We get all their questions on the table again. What is expected of a church planter? What does it really mean to seek God? What does it mean to disciple? What is involved in building community? What does it mean to win the lost? How committed is the student to an internal motivation? We do additional Biblical word studies, a study dealing with grace versus law, and another on the integrity of Scripture. We want our church planters to be people who are not merely parroting what we do. We want them to be living out of their own convictions. We develop tailor-made training for the particular nation or location where they will be planting a church. Finally, when they have completed our process, the team is blessed by our congregation and they are sent out to plant a new church."[12]

This training process has enabled members of Antioch Community Church to be released to start ten new churches in three years. Nine of those new church plants are in nations and among people groups whose exposure to the Gospel has been very limited, if not absent. As God burdens the hearts of Antioch members for people groups around the world, their training school is prepared to equip members to be sent as carriers of the Gospel among those peoples.

One limitation of spontaneous multiplication of new churches is trained leadership. Traditional training models are designed to add leaders who have completed extensive training. The number of new leaders who graduate from traditional seminaries and Bible colleges each year remains relatively consistent. It is impossible to experience exponential growth in new churches if new leaders are emerging only at an additive rate. Addition cannot keep pace with multiplication. If for no other reason than this, the church must consider its unique role in providing alternative training processes for members whom God is sending in mission.

Multiplying congregations are taking new forms, and their leadership requires new preparation for ministry. To plant churches and incorporate new disciples into effective relational systems, house or simple churches are burgeoning. Relinquishing the distinction between laity and clergy (a most unfortunate albatross born out of the period called Christendom), house church leaders require a new form of equipping and preparation.

The systems designed to meet their needs are likely to include just-in-time training rather than that typically prescribed in a standard training curriculum. House church advocate Wolfgang Simson shares a vision for one hundred million churches to be planted in this generation. He poses the question, "How do we train Christians to become planters of healthy networks of house churches? We need a few dozen millions. How can disciples be trained in a multipliable and healthy way that does not mix their mission with ambitious motives, fleshly desires, denominational interests, nor the building of small empires?"[13]

Even the casual observer would identify the improbable potential of today's formal training structures to equip "a few dozen millions" to serve this generation. As in the Old Testament paradigm, student prophets gained mental and spiritual training from their observation of senior prophets, not in withdrawal from the world but in the context of ministry in the world (1 Samuel 19:20; 1 Kings 20:35; 2 Kings 2:3–7; 4:38–44). So, in the New Testament, the apostles learned as they observed the daily activities of the one called Rabbi or Teacher. Subsequently, those apostles were paired with others who would graduate from another on-the-job academy. Multiplying leadership can only be accomplished in the context of ministry, not in isolation from it. This training is best accomplished as the local church equips its members through ministry to be released to ministry.

They See Multiplication as God's Design for Reaching New Generations

Missional churches seek to be shaped by God's heart. They are indwelt by the power of His Spirit and live in a world that is profoundly spiritual, but often without knowledge of the one true God. In a sense, missional churches are like a pneumatic tire, inflated with air pressure that is highly concentrated within its closed environment. If a nail penetrates the closed environment, the air rushes out and the tire goes flat. But what causes the air to be released? The fact that the pressure on the inside is greater than the pressure on the outside.

Similarly, the missional church—operating in the power of the Spirit—is highly charged. Its members possess a power far beyond anything the world affords. This creates a constant tension to release the Spirit into the world's vacuum. If every church were involved in this releasing activity, a rapid multiplication of New Testament congregations would disciple the countless millions of persons responding to the fresh wind of God's Spirit. Those new churches would be in every nation, among every people group, and every socioeconomic spectrum of society. Those churches would cover the earth just as the waters cover the sea, "For the earth will be filled with the knowledge of the glory of the Lord" (Habakkuk 2:14) and "All the ends of the earth will remember and turn to the Lord, and all the families of the nations will worship" (Psalm 22:27).

It is to this end that missional churches release their members in local ministries, in short-term mission projects, and as church planters throughout the nations. These churches understand multiplication as God's design for reaching new generations. Their concern is not to become megachurches, but to be multiplying churches. Because there are people living near them who desire to experience worship differently, they start new churches within their own community. They start churches not because those people would not be welcomed into the existing church, but because the sponsor church's format of worship would not address the longing of their souls.

Charles Chaney has spent a lifetime studying church starting in America. He has frequently heard the challenges raised in opposition to church planting: there are empty seats in virtually every church in the nation. We do not need more churches; we just need to fill up the ones we have. To such challenges, Chaney has responded, "America will not be won to Christ by existing churches, [or] by establishing more churches like the vast majority of those we now have. . . . We should give attention to multiplying congregations among all the social and cultural segments of society."[14]

Without regard to locations, missional churches are actively releasing members to new ministries and new churches. Their passion is to see the people of all nations worship God. Because the task is great, missional churches grasp the principles of multiplication. The task is too great for any individual church. It is too great for all the churches existing today. But the task of global missions is not too big for the grandchurches and great-grandchurches planted by today's churches. Missional churches are not simply releasing members to start churches. Their focus is on starting church-starting movements. Releasing members to start new churches is addition. Releasing members to start church-planting churches results in movements. Movements practice multiplication. The members of Antioch Community Church do not simply plant churches; they plant churches that start their own church planter training schools. They fully intend to plant church-starting churches. In fact, Seibert's goal for the next fifteen years is for Antioch to plant two hundred churches that do their own movements.

This vision reflects a new paradigm for success. Concerning measures of success, Tinsley wrote, "The measure of church success may need to be reevaluated. One day, a church may evaluate its fulfillment of Christ's commission not only on the basis of attendance, its strength of fellowship, budget and cash flow, but by the number of congregations it begets."[15] Indeed, missional churches are redefining what it means to be a church. Seibert says that missional churches believe "everything that has life reproduces itself. Once a person is born again, they reproduce life in others through evangelism and discipleship. Small groups reproduce and grow churches. And when churches reproduce churches, they produce movements. The missional church has no lower goal than movements of people across the earth reaching those who have never heard, until all hear."

Missional churches are growing. Many of them are growing numerically. As members live in intimacy with God as authentic disciples, living and proclaiming His kingdom, they draw others toward themselves and toward God. Others come into the fellowship as new followers of Christ. From the moment they come in, they are being equipped to go back out. Missional churches measure their growth by their capacity to release rather than retain.

Reflection and Application

1. Enlist leaders to observe an instructional lab associated with a trade school or profession. Observe the various pedagogical methods used in that training. Encourage the group to use their observations to develop a new disciple-equipping model that incorporates their insights. Ask them to create the model as though neither money nor expertise were an object. Ultimately, determine how their new creation can inform the church's equipping process.

2. Visit the Percept Website (www.percept.info.com) or contact judicatory offices to obtain demographic information for the area where your church has its primary ministry. Use the information to identify segments of the population that may not be reached by existing churches. Ask a group of leaders to consider potential ministries to which those people might respond. Consider how comfortable they might be in uniting with your church. Is it possible your church might begin a new church to more adequately include them?

3. Obtain a list of all church members and the ministry roles served by each. Identify those ministries that primarily reach out to nonmembers and those that primarily meet members' needs. Assess the balance of ministry between the two areas of focus. Suggest a worship service in which all those serving in ministry would be commissioned, either as those serving the church (commissioned to pastoral care and equipping) or those reaching beyond the church (serving in mission and ministry).

SUGGESTED READING

Hockin-Boyd, C., and Minatrea, M. (eds.). *Hands on Ministry: Pastoral Care Training for Volunteers*. Dallas: Baptist General Convention of Texas, 1998.

Schwab, A. W. *When the Members Are the Missionaries: An Extraordinary Calling for Ordinary People*. Essex, N.Y.: Member Mission Press, 2002.

Van Engen, C. *God's Missionary People: Rethinking the Purpose of the Local Church*. Grand Rapids, Mich.: Baker Book House, 1991.

Missional Practice Assessment

Rate each statement that follows from 1 (the statement is not true of our church) to 7 (the statement is true of our church) by circling the appropriate response. The greatest insight will be gained if you avoid selecting 4 as a response. Please use that selection minimally. When you are finished, transfer your responses to the assessments in the Appendix and total your scores to find your net response. Your group's response to these assessments gives a clear picture of your church's readiness to move to being missional.

We consider it a blessing when we give members to start new churches or ministries.

| 1 | 2 | 3 | 4 | 5 | 6 | 7 |

Our church equips disciples to serve as missionaries.

| 1 | 2 | 3 | 4 | 5 | 6 | 7 |

Our members believe new churches are needed in our community.

| 1 | 2 | 3 | 4 | 5 | 6 | 7 |

We expect members to be "on mission" locally and globally.

| 1 | 2 | 3 | 4 | 5 | 6 | 7 |

We regularly commission members who are going into ministry.

| 1 | 2 | 3 | 4 | 5 | 6 | 7 |

Our church has an aggressive plan for starting new community ministries and churches.

| 1 | 2 | 3 | 4 | 5 | 6 | 7 |

We successfully move new believers into leadership roles.

| 1 | 2 | 3 | 4 | 5 | 6 | 7 |

MISSIONAL PRACTICE NUMBER NINE

PLACE KINGDOM CONCERNS FIRST

But seek first the kingdom of God and His righteousness,
and all these things shall be added to you.

—Matthew 6:33

When the Kingdom of God comes, it comes with fire.
It flows like a river of molten lava, consuming every stronghold
of the enemy. No institution or sector is left unaffected.

—George Otis Jr., Foreword, *City Reaching*

CHRISTIANS OF DIFFERENT DENOMINATIONS often find themselves involved in skirmishes over practice and belief. But as Christians, it is fundamental to remember that we are not each other's enemies; we have a common enemy who stands opposed to righteousness.

Matt Hannan of New Heights puts it succinctly: "We are not in competition with other believers. We do not have to fight with one another. We are not marking our territory and prohibiting others from ministering there. We are in this Kingdom together. So it's not all about routing people into our church as *the church*. We want people to get into the church where they can feel comfortable and grow. We count it a success if we help someone to begin growing as a disciple anywhere."[1]

Missional church members continually find that they must wrestle with these critical questions:

- How can we develop Kingdom disciples, people who can evidence what the world would look like if God were revered as King?
- How can we cooperate rather than competing, embracing, living, and moving comfortably among believers of different denominations?
- How can we stand for right and oppose every evil that prevents others from experiencing the joy of Kingdom living?

There is an authentic battle raging in the spiritual realm, and it is a Kingdom matter. I cannot underscore this point too strongly: no significant Kingdom accomplishment will occur until churches value Kingdom more than their own sectarian accomplishments. Missional churches seek to raise the standard of the cross in territories currently occupied by forces of the enemy. Though they value their beliefs, they are passionate about the Kingdom of God. Although there may be many denominational expressions, there is but one ensign under which they serve. Wherever it is raised, the cross evidences the defeat of the prince of the darkness and victory for the King of Righteousness. A kingdom can have multiple princes, but only one king. Although another prince battles for its dominion, ultimately all of creation belongs to one King, is part of one kingdom. The church serves as the contemporary representative of that kingdom, the Kingdom of God.

C. S. Lewis referred to the world as "enemy-occupied territory" and Christianity as "the story of how the rightful king has landed, you might say landed in disguise, and is calling us to take part in a great campaign of sabotage."[2] The mission of God brings His presence to occupy territory the enemy desires to rule. The occupation of the Kingdom of God occurs in four domains: within believers, in the church, over all creation, and over principalities and powers in the spiritual realm. This four-sphere model builds upon the work of Oscar Cullman and Charles Van Engen, as shown in Figure 11.1.

This model expresses several important ideas:

- Jesus taught "the Kingdom of God is within you" (Luke 17:21). The Kingdom is both a gift received and a realm entered by disciples of

Figure 11.1. The Domains of Christ's Rule in the Kingdom of God.

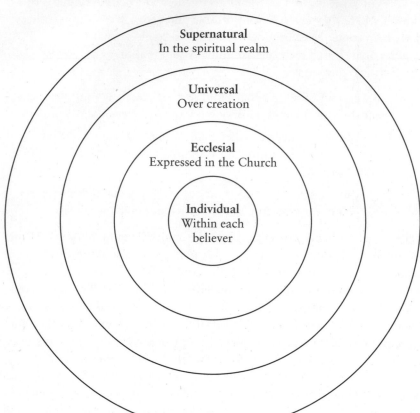

Supernatural
In the spiritual realm

Universal
Over creation

Ecclesial
Expressed in the Church

Individual
Within each
believer

Christ, and it exists within every believer. This is the Individual realm of
God's reign.

• Every believer is part of the Body of Christ, the church. Although the
church and the Kingdom of God are not synonymous, the church is a current expression of the Kingdom of God. The church is the corporate
domain of the Kingdom, identified as the Ecclesial Reign of God. It serves as
a present-day expression of the eschatological reality promised in Scripture.

• God's reign extends to all creation. All of creation awaits the eschatological moment when all that is wrong shall be set right; "all creation
groans . . . awaiting the day of redemption" (Romans 8:22–23). God's
reign over creation is His Universal reign.

• His Kingdom reign also extends over invisible thrones and domin-
ions, rulers and authorities—the unseen spiritual realm (Colossians

1:16–17). Although not visible to the church, it is in this conflicted realm that battles for spiritual supremacy and authority are waged and in which Christ's resurrection ensured His ultimate and final victory. This is God's reign over the Supernatural realm.

It is in these four domains that missional churches focus their efforts. They represent the Kingdom of God as they invite individuals to surrender their lives to the Kingdom reign of Christ as Lord. Together with other believers, they make up an outpost of the Kingdom, the local church, and together with other congregations they make up the catholic church at large. As stewards of God's creation, missional communities model righteous concern for all creation, caring for rather than abusing those things His hands have made. Finally, through intercessory prayer, the missional church tears down strongholds raised up against the knowledge and reign of God in the unseen world.

In their passion for the Kingdom of God, missional churches serve to ensure that every person has the opportunity to respond to the King's invitation, becoming part of the Kingdom. They see themselves as only one battalion of a great kingdom force deployed on earth. Other Christians are brothers and sisters serving the same master. Although their affiliation might be with different denominations, they find their primary identity as part of the Kingdom. They distinguish between essentials and nonessentials in doctrinal interpretation, value and cooperate with Christians from other traditions in Kingdom tasks, and join together in spiritual warfare against the enemy. These are the intentions of missional churches:

- Missional churches seek to develop Kingdom citizens.
- Missional churches seek to express the Kingdom of God in the world.
- Missional churches cooperate, not compete, in the Kingdom of God.
- Missional churches battle a common enemy.

Missional Churches Seek to Develop Kingdom Citizens

During His earthly ministry, Jesus' primary message revolved around the Kingdom of God. He revealed that personal entrance into the Kingdom was accomplished through the miracle of being born again (John 3:3). Many of his parables provided insight concerning life in the Kingdom. Through them, followers learned how to live as Kingdom citizens. The Sermon on the Mount is a primer on life in the Kingdom of God.

NorthWood Church for the Communities is committed to helping members apply the Sermon on the Mount in daily living, developing members as kingdom pilgrims. Their strategy emphasizes glocal participation in the Kingdom of God as pilgrims who are on journey doing the will of God. New-member training includes four distinct engagements of God's reign among NorthWood members: the Body, the family, the nation, and the world. A philosophical summary of NorthWood's vision is stated as "Kingdom In—Kingdom Out." The staff is committed to equipping members for their roles in God's Kingdom. They are striving to develop and use a vocabulary of the Kingdom. Rather than directing the focus toward themselves as the local church, NorthWood seeks to redirect the focus of the church toward the Kingdom. Members are asked to make an annual commitment of themselves as Kingdom Pilgrims empowered by the Holy Spirit who will:

- Aggressively, internally pursue the Kingdom of God here and now
- Be a part of the prayer ministry
- Be in ongoing community in an adult team
- Share their faith weekly
- Give financially sacrificially
- Serve consistently in ministry
- Help with three special events during the year
- Learn and apply one new discipline to life during the year

Literature published by the church reminds readers that NorthWood is on a "Kingdom Pilgrim Journey" and encourages all disciples to find and fulfill their role in the Kingdom. Every member is encouraged to hear and pursue God's direction as an authentic disciple on mission in the revolutionary agenda of the Kingdom of God. They are to listen daily for the voice of God as they worship. Their personal relationship with God evidences their citizenship. François Fenelon regarded the Kingdom of God as His impenetrable presence within believers: "It does not take much time to love God, in order to renew ourselves in his presence, to raise our hearts to him or to worship him in the depths of our heart, to offer him what we do and what we suffer. That is the true kingdom of God within us, which nothing can disturb."[3] NorthWood believes as members are renewed in their relationship with God and are equipped for Kingdom living (Kingdom In), their lives will consistently reflect Kingdom values (Kingdom Out).

The Kingdom within will manifest itself in the external activities of disciples. Jamye Miller believes Kingdom disciples share a DNA that guides their actions: "At one level it is the whole shift into the Kingdom, coming under the Lord's authority. We have to get up each day and say, 'Lord here I am and I want to be absolutely yours today.' Western Christians are steeped in independence, rather than in submission to authority."[4] To follow Christ means to let go of our prerogatives, just as Christ did in the incarnation. It is to demonstrate what God is really like and live His will—to demonstrate His Kingdom in the world. Letting go of personal prerogatives while submitting to those of God will result in Kingdom disciples who faithfully invite others into the Kingdom. Kingdom living is first about purpose and value. It asks, "What is on the heart of God?" Then it is the sending of God's people to where they are supposed to be. It is everybody a missionary. In each disciple's *oikos* (sphere of influence), he or she will ask, "How can I bring the influence, the reign, and the authority of God to bear here so that people can know Him and glorify Him the way He deserves to be glorified?"

Miller elaborates: "Life begets life. Living things multiply. It is a principle of the Kingdom of God, and it is a nonnegotiable. You have to believe that at your core. It works in biological terms, in cellular language and more profoundly in spiritual terms. If it is true, in the Kingdom, that life begets life, then for me as an individual, I am going to find a way to share this wonderful life that is within me and see that life reproduced. Healthy believers reproduce believers."[5] As disciples following a King on a mission, there is no choice. It is absolutely and utterly unavoidable that his followers be totally given, sold out, and set apart to do His purpose. They cannot describe who they are apart from the Lord's Kingdom purpose for them on earth.

Kingdom disciples live between the historic "already" and the "not yet" of God's drama of redemption. Because of their relationship with Christ, they have become part of His eternal Kingdom and servants in His church. They invite others to experience relationship with Him. At the same time, they are not yet totally free from the effects of sin. They seek to do the will of the Father, but they also experience temptation to pursue their own desires. They know the historic battle to which the Apostle Paul referred when he said, "For the good that I wish, I do not do; but I practice the very evil that I do not wish. . . . I find then the principle that evil is present in me, the one who wishes to do good" (Romans 7:19, 21). Kingdom disciples live transparent lives, acknowledging the struggles they face in living consistently the values of the Kingdom. Their admissions of vulnerability, rather than detracting from their effective witness, validate the authenticity of their position as followers of the King *on the way to* the Kingdom. Christ has already become the Lord of their lives, but they are not yet all they shall be. They invite others to join them as followers of the King, to experience His grace and mercy.

Individual servants are the building blocks of the Kingdom. Though they possess a passion to see the King worshipped, they do not draw attention to themselves as they extend His invitation. They are thrilled to lose their identity into the One whose Kingdom they have entered. Wolfgang Simson refers to these passionate disciples as present-day "Knoxers," after John Knox, whose consuming desire and prayer for the lost of his nation was, "Give me Scotland, 'ere I die." Of these followers Simson said: "God begins His movements with people who care not that their names are known. They have a passion to see God's Kingdom realized in their world. Usually they are not recognized or embraced people. They are generally ignored by their peers and are sometimes thought strange."[6]

Whether they are thought strange or not, the humility of Kingdom servants erases self-concern. Bob Roberts describes his aspirations for the future: "My passion is to be part of a movement in the Kingdom of God that is so powerful that when historians study it—unlike past movements, no single individual will emerge. Instead, after study and evaluation, they will say what took place was not because of any one of them, but because of all of them."[7]

Each disciple comes into the Kingdom individually. Yet as he or she enters the Kingdom, each becomes part of the larger Body of Christ. Unfortunately, many Western Christians prioritize the personal implications of their entrance into the Kingdom while failing to value the corporate implications of the same. George R. Hunsberger addresses this dichotomy: "The church has tended to separate the news of the reign of God from God's provision for humanity's salvation. This separation has made salvation a private event by dividing 'my personal salvation' from the advent of God's healing reign over all the world."[8] Essentially, he points out, salvation is both personal and communal. Individually, those who respond to the Gospel receive the gift of the reign of Jesus Christ as Lord. Communally, in salvation they come into the Kingdom of God, becoming part of the realm in which God reigns. Thus the reign of God is both "a gift one receives and a realm one enters."[9]

With regard to its communal nature, the church must reclaim the implications of being a community of authentic disciples. Through their shared experiences, members of the Body of Christ influence social structures and public life with values that find their source in Kingdom ethic. The church lives the Gospel; "the Kingdom of God is among you." It does not simply proclaim the Gospel. By its lifestyle, the church authenticates a value system different from self-serving secularism.

Missional Churches Seek to Express the Kingdom of God in the World

The church is sown in the soil of human hearts of all the continents of the world, among diverse political systems and various economic orders. Into this diversity the church introduces a single kingdom whose values supersede all worldly systems. In *City of God, City of Satan,* Robert Linthicum comments that because the church is not historically connected with any one political or economic system, it is not limited to any one place. "Rather," he says, "throughout the whole world, wherever God's people may be found, the kingdom of God is growing and advancing in all governments and in spite of those governments."[10]

It may appear overly optimistic, but this assessment of the influential potential of the kingdom of God afforded through the church is unexaggerated. Missional churches are involved in making lives better, enhancing the quality of life for those in the communities where those churches are located and to the ends of the earth. They do this as they pursue all the interests of the Redeemer's Kingdom through the Body of Christ. The missional church blesses the world through its presence. Its community is a better place to live because the church is there. It provides viable evidence of the power of God to transform societies through the actions of transformed individuals. According to *Planning Strategies for World Evangelization,* "The church's mission is its participation in and cooperation with what God is graciously doing redemptively here on earth. The church is to be a sign and a sacrament of the presence of the kingdom in word and deed. It is to be a partial answer to the prayer, 'Thy Kingdom come, thy will be done, on earth as it is in heaven.'"[11]

As it lives missionally in fulfillment of its purpose, the church has an impact on the world in a variety of ways. When its members' lives are fashioned by kingdom values, their workplaces are positively influenced. Through caring ministries, disenfranchised people find help and hope. As dialogue ensues among those who have experienced the practical holiness and applied Christianity of disciples, explanation and invitation to become part of the Kingdom result in new disciples being birthed. Although it is the church deployed into the world, it represents more than just the church. The church represents the King and the Kingdom He came proclaiming in His incarnation.

As he addresses urban issues, Linthicum says "God's primary intention for the city is . . . to permeate its political, economic, and religious structures, to transform the lives of its inhabitants, to exorcise evil and unrepentant principalities and powers and to place over that city . . .

Christ."[12] Were the church to accomplish the desire of God's heart, every city would display the character of God, evidence of His reign. To that purpose, the church is sent into the world. This is still the dream. Unfortunately, the presence of churches in an area does not ensure a clear representation of the Kingdom. Western churches have often allowed their calendars to be filled with many activities that expend the energy of the Body without leading to accomplishment of God's missional purpose. They give members the opportunity for social interaction, recreation, and sporting events. Sundays may be given not only to church school, Bible study, and worship but to numerous additional committee meetings required to oversee internal care issues, property management, and program continuation. Additional offerings during the week are designed to address areas of special interest among members, or they are used for rehearsals of groups that will lead in upcoming worship services.

Even though each of these activities may be worthy of attention, and churches seldom go out of their way to include unworthy activities, the good remains the enemy of the best. It is distinctly possible to fill every available moment of the church calendar with opportunities that would never result in announcement of the reign of God. Mission can be subsumed in a menagerie of good activities that compete with missional activities for the limited time members give their church.

Missional Churches Cooperate, Not Compete, in the Kingdom of God

The Kingdom of God is in competition with manifold activities, and its message can be obscured as a lost world tries to choose among the various denominational affiliations. Though Jesus prayed to the Father "that they may be One even as we are one, that the world may know that you sent me," the church is anything but "one." Scripture interpretation varies, so we naturally gather with those who believe as we do. Too often, Christian leaders impose their own interpretations as critical. Ultimately, they draw lines indicating "acceptable" interpretation of Scripture. Those whose practices differ are excluded. To quote Riddell, "the church struggles to become what it in essence is"[13] and in so doing creates distance.

Missional churches see this problem quite clearly and attempt to remove all barriers that hinder access to the Kingdom. Even the Gospel is identified as a "stumbling block" over which some struggle to pass. Missional churches avoid adding nonessentials that may become stumbling blocks to those receiving their presentation of the Gospel.

Jeff Harris emphasized this concern: "We are not into acrostics. We do not list our denominational affiliation or its abbreviation on our signs or publicity. A lost world does not understand the existence of all the different denominations, much less the various brands of Baptists or Presbyterians. We try to remain apolitical regarding denominational issues. We do not see their emphasis helping us to effectively reach people with the Gospel."[14] Grace Point values its interpretation of historic beliefs, but even so the church simplifies its message to those who are not part of the church. It removes potential barriers rather than raising them.

This matter is critical to mission in a rapidly shrinking world. Regrettably, Western Christianity has often mingled nonessential cultural practices with the Gospel in mission efforts. This has resulted in promoting nonindigenous practices among developing churches. Subsequent evangelization by those churches then requires potential believers to adopt what they often view as a foreign faith.

Where the church has developed without the attachments of other cultures, indigenous practices enhance interpretation of the Gospel. This is in part why indigenous churches in the Southern Hemisphere are multiplying believers at rates far exceeding the Western church. The time is past when missionaries were sent predominantly from Western churches to Southern nations. Today, Southern Hemisphere churches are sending missionaries to Europe and North America. In the words of David Bosch, "Everywhere the church is in the diaspora, in a situation of mission."[15] The shrinking globe and activities of God's Spirit have resulted in new cooperation in the enterprise of the Kingdom of God. Ted Ward, considering implications for mission agencies in a changing world, wrote: "When the contrast between Christian and Muslim or Christian and Buddhist is at stake, the label 'Presbyterian' does not help much. In today's world many Christians find it far more important to identify with other Christians precisely because they need to stand together as Christians."[16]

Nearly two hundred years ago, Barton W. Stone, one of the founders of the American Restoration Movement, verbalized what was to become his life ambition: "Let Christian unity be our polar star."[17] Later, Carl Ketcherside would communicate the same vision: "Wherever God has a child, I have a brother or sister."[18]

Missional churches resonate with these statements. They view other churches in their area not as competitors but as members of the same team. They hold a high view of the corporate Body of Christ, the composite of all churches. Missional churches are often at the forefront of city-reaching movements. These movements call the entire Body of Christ together in a geographical area to pray, partner, encourage, and support the common purposes of the Kingdom in their locale. It is not uncommon to see such churches identify themselves as "a part of the Body of Christ in (a particular city and state)." Although they continue to value their individual beliefs and interpretations of Scripture, they publicly identify with other churches in the community.

New Heights Church exemplifies this spirit of cooperation through various means. Those attending worship at New Heights receive a printed worship folder and a weekly "fridge flyer." Designed to be taken home and placed on the refrigerator door, the fridge flyer communicates "news you can use." It reminds members of ministry opportunities, upcoming events, and prayer concerns every time they open their refrigerator door. A typical inclusion in the fridge flyer requests prayer for community churches: "While praying for New Heights, please pray for these churches and their pastors as well: First Congregational, Ed Evans; Good Shepherd Lutheran, Tom Moeller; Parkside Church, Darryl Elledge; Salmon Creek United Methodist, J. Michael Graef. God is building His Church by using *many* congregations in our community."[19]

The cooperative spirit is not just rhetoric at New Heights. The church's intern process for church planters is not limited to those affiliated with a single denominational tradition. Their investments in church starting include Lutheran, Methodist, and Episcopal churches, among others. Those churches are located not only in the northwest but around the world. A former exchange student from Slovakia visited New Heights and ultimately became a follower of Christ. Upon his return to Slovakia, he sensed God's direction to become a pastor or church planter. Over a number of years, New Heights has continued to invest in his preparation by assisting his attendance at a Slovakian Lutheran seminary, enabling his return to participate in New Height's church-planting intern training process, and providing a residence where he and his wife can mentor other evangelical leaders.

A liberating simplicity is found among churches that remove barriers and rejoice in cooperation with other Kingdom citizens. They accept the words of Jesus: "he who is not against you is for you" (Luke 9:50).

Missional Churches Battle a Common Enemy

Since they are not in competition with one another, missional churches can stand together opposing a common enemy as they seek the transformation of their communities. Their vision is a moment-by-moment, day-by-day shifting of balance in power and control from the domain of Satan to the Kingdom of God. Missional churches are involved in the ongoing battle against the "prince of the power of the air" whose influence is disobedience to Christ and who has "blinded the minds of the unbelieving, that they might not see the light of the gospel of the glory of Christ" (Ephesians 2:2; 2 Corinthians 4:4). Their enemy is not human, not of flesh, but spiritual. Therefore their battle weapons are not physical, but spiritual, "divinely powerful for the destruction of fortresses" (2 Corinthians 10:4).

Missional churches practice prayer as a tool of spiritual warfare. The priority of prayer among these churches is evidenced in members' participation in intercessory prayer, extensive time in prayer vigils, prayer walking, spiritual mapping, and prayer journaling. Because they are attuned to global issues, daily news reports serve as catalysts for prayer among missional church members as they recognize the profound impact international events and the decisions of international leaders have on the cause of Christ and His Kingdom. Missional churches are in the business of praying "Thy Kingdom come, Thy will be done on earth." Through prayer, they seek His Kingdom purpose in the world.

Prayer is not the only means through which missional churches confront the enemy. Of equal importance is what they do after they have prayed, as members empowered by the Spirit exhibit holiness and compassion in their daily lives. Transformed believers can transform society. As members carry the influence of the Gospel into their individual spheres of influence, spiritual victories are accomplished. City-reaching leader and practitioner Jim Herrington advocates the significant role given each believer in penetrating his or her city with the transforming power of Christ: "Transformation is an *inside-out* and *downside-up* process. . . . Clearly, when a sufficient number of believers become mature, dynamic disciples of Christ, their presence in government, the arts, business, and other systems in society should be felt—*will* be felt."[20]

What is true of a city is also true of a state, nation, or world. Society is influenced as missional churches equip and release members to be the presence of Christ in their spheres of influence. Their impact is referred to by Christ in parable as the "leaven" that ultimately leavens all (Matthew 13:33). The Kingdom of God claims victory over the enemy through the leavened lives of missional Christians. Together, those believers display God's intended design for creation. They are a present-day reflection of the eternal reign of Christ, the future reality. In the creative expression of Craig Van Gelder, borrowed from a farming practice designed to get farmers to use innovations in agriculture, it is "God's demonstration plot in the world. Its very existence demonstrates that his redemptive reign has already begun. Its very presence invites the world to watch, listen, examine, and consider accepting God's reign as a superior way of living."[21]

Missional churches are God's demonstration plots. They reveal the Kingdom of God into which each believer has been placed. Together believers constitute the church of Jesus Christ, a community of the Kingdom. Missional churches cooperate with other believers in pursuit of the interests of the Redeemer's Kingdom. They are not in competition with one another; rather, they stand united in opposition to the one who, through lies and schemes, seeks to divert others from the Kingdom. They value their beliefs, although they do not agree in every area of interpretation. They do not focus their passion on what separates them, but on that which unites them: the Kingdom of God. Missional churches are not building *their* kingdoms. Their primary allegiance is to *His* Kingdom.

Reflection and Application

1. Encourage members to identify and submit short phrases communicating Kingdom values. Enlist a group of highly creative persons to develop an "ad campaign" through which members will be exposed to Kingdom values for everyday living. Plan a sermon series to complement the emphasis.

2. Visit the Dawn Ministries Website (www.dawnministries.org/regions/nam/index.html). Which Kingdom strategies delineated there parallel your church's concerns? Brainstorm ways in which your purpose and strategic plan contribute to a Kingdom vision.

3. Move outside your tradition in experiencing worship. Ask God to reveal Himself through elements of worship with which you are not familiar or comfortable. Journal emotions, feelings, sensory responses, and insights you realized during those worship experiences. Consider how practices of various traditions are windows through which God reaches into the heart. What new experiences could be introduced into your church's worship?

Suggested Reading (and Viewing)

Dennison, J. *City Reaching: On the Road to Community Transformation.* Pasadena, Calif.: William Carey Library, 1999.

Sentinel Group. *Transformations I and II.* (Available on video and CD.) P.O. Box 6334, Lynnwood, WA 98036; (800) 668-5657; Web: http://www.sentinelgroup.org/)

Missional Practice Assessment

Rate each statement that follows from 1 (the statement is not true of our church) to 7 (the statement is true of our church) by circling the appropriate response. The greatest insight will be gained if you avoid selecting 4 as a response. Please use that selection minimally. When you are finished, transfer your responses to the assessments in the Appendix and total your scores to find your net response. Your group's response to these assessments give a clear picture of your church's readiness to move to being missional.

Our actions evidence our partnership with Christian churches in our community.

1   2   3   4   5   6   7

We emphasize the communal as well as individual nature of salvation.

1   2   3   4   5   6 .   7

We share the pain and joy of Christians around the world.

1   2   3   4   5   6   7

We intentionally partner with all believers in the work of the Kingdom.

1   2   3   4   5   6   7

In worship we regularly pray for other churches in our city.

1   2   3   4   5   6   7

Members participate in spiritual warfare through a vital prayer ministry.

1   2   3   4   5   6   7

Our members are involved in interdenominational ministries.

1   2   3   4   5   6   7

PART THREE

STRUCTURES AND STRATEGIES FOR BECOMING MISSIONAL

Wake up, and strengthen the things that remain,
which were about to die; for I have not found
your deeds completed in the sight of My God.

—Revelation 3:2

MUCH HAS BEEN WRITTEN about the pervasive changes relative to the missional task of churches in recent decades. The dissolution of Christendom has been acknowledged, sometimes with angst, other times with elation. Some bemoan loss of the former bias that the church once enjoyed; others acknowledge the incapacity of faith to transform, unless it is validated as authentic when proven in the fabric of pluralism. Authentic faith rises to the surface in the face of conflict and challenge. No longer assumed to be the faith of choice, Christianity must again prove its worth in answering the deepest questions of the human heart with clarity and power.

In a society that values religious pluralism and tolerance, the Christian church cannot assume that its message is automatically received with joy. In many realms, the claims of Christ carry no greater weight than do the tenets of Islam, Hinduism, Buddhism, or Taoism. The assumption that any one religion has a lock on truth is rejected outright. Rapids of religious pluralism flood bookshelves, airwaves, and office conversations. Social propriety demands allowance that truth may be found among all the major religious traditions, all reflecting various pathways to the same God. Others decry the existence of any God as an archaic retention of past ages, when what could not be clarified by science was consigned to the actions of deity. It is assumed the advances of humanity have lessened the need for mythical explication of that which was once mysterious.

Missional church structures must equip and empower disciples for a buoyant apologetic that rises to the surface amid pluralistic turbulence. Opportunities to communicate truth arise when others observe the acceptance, service, and authenticity displayed in the lives of disciples. This is why missional churches prioritize the development of structures that prepare disciples for the missional task. In this final part, we look at how churches can modify their existing structures and leadership patterns to thrive in this new world.

THEY RUN RAPIDS IN RUBBER RAFTS

CHURCH STRUCTURES THAT CAN SURVIVE THE RAPIDS OF CULTURAL CHANGE

And He was saying to them, "The Sabbath was made for man, and not man for the Sabbath."

—Mark 2:27

We have awakened to a world in which the mission frontier has changed. The organization and the structure of church life, formed for that one mission, now need to be reoriented to face the new frontier.

—Loren B. Mead, *The Once and Future Church*

WHITEWATER RAFTING is a popular recreational activity for thrill seekers and adventure enthusiasts. The sport has even been adopted in corporate learning adventures for team building. Why? Because working as a team is not optional in whitewater: rafters must react quickly to commands given by the person responsible for guiding their craft. The best whitewater rafters are those who have learned to trust the directions given, the sufficiency of their skills for the task, and the complementary function of others on their team. The construction of the raft itself is of utmost importance. Rocked by powerful forces, crashing wildly against rocks, the only way to survive is in a craft flexible enough to withstand the constant pounding. Where a rigid vessel would soon break apart, rubber rafts are flexible and resilient.

This is an apt metaphor for churches as they attempt to navigate the rapids of social and cultural change taking place today. We must work as a faithful team, and our churches must have flexible and resilient structures that allow us to encounter, influence, evangelize, equip, and empower people effectively as authentic disciples sent into the rapids of societal change as emissaries of God.

Rejuvenating Aging Church Structures

Among the most commonly observed debilitating conditions of the elderly is osteoporosis, a condition characterized by bones that become brittle and increasingly liable to fracture. Observers of churches often note similarities between this condition in aging physical structures and aging ecclesial structures. A person with osteoporosis is less able to withstand physical trauma, a fall, a twisted ankle, or a striking blow. Aging church structures are often rigid, brittle, and inflexible, unable to adapt to their changing environments. In fact, a church might well move to avoid contact with the culture outside the church, sensing its inability to adapt to the stresses associated with such exposure.

Consultants who assist churches in strategic planning often find structural inflexibility and rigidity that negate the church's capacity to adapt to cultural change. Constitutions and bylaws, policies and procedures, rather than being dynamic documents designed to change with changing times, may become unchanged verbalizations of "the way we do things around here." Organizational structures once fashioned to accommodate the influx of new people in a growing congregation can become impediments consuming the church's energy in maintenance, long beyond their effectiveness. In communities where significant transition has occurred, it is not unusual to find churches that once numbered three hundred people or more now reduced to seventy or eighty active members. Amazingly, those churches may still try to fill every slot in an organizational and committee structure created during the former era. A church with seventy people and seventeen committees has come to view structure as sacred.

When so much is invested in structures, people tend to seek their preservation. But a high level of investment and commitment to structures can in no way ensure they will still be functional tomorrow. Their preservation may do nothing to connect the church with its rapidly changing environment.

Missional churches take another approach. They seek to create low-investment structures and keep their mission and purpose as the priority. Their structures must be flexible, capable of adapting quickly to the changing opportunities their context brings to the missional purpose. Thus missional communities often possess significantly fewer long-term structural designs than conventional churches.

For instance, rather than developing ongoing committee structures with rotation systems for members, missional churches might form task-related teams that dissolve when their assignment has been completed. In some instances, missional churches decide to be tabernacle rather than temple congregations. They prefer to be mobile, using leased or borrowed facilities, or members' homes, rather than purchasing properties and buildings. Some congregations that own facilities have agreed not to erect additional buildings as they continue to grow. Instead, their intent is to release members to start new churches and ministries. Rather than celebrating increased *building* capacity, they celebrate increased *releasing* capacity. Driven by the understanding of mission, such decisions affect church structure.

Mission Structures and Missional Churches

Conventional churches often have mission programs as part of their congregational structure. They may include age-level organizations whose purpose is to promote mission education and raise support. During the modern missions era, these structures developed to allow church members to be informed about the activities of missionaries they supported who were serving in distant locations. At the beginning of the last century, travel to foreign places was difficult, dangerous, and time consuming for most church members. But in today's global environment, where church members regularly travel between nations for business purposes, formerly effective missions programs struggle to find their place in contemporary structures.

Missional churches perceive missions not as a program of the church, but as the essence of the church. Therefore every component of the church's identity relates to its missional purpose. No longer a single compartment within the church's structure, missional churches expect every task of the church to be informed by the church's missional purpose. Few missional churches relegate oversight of their participation in missions to a special "missions committee" operating on a budget and in a realm separate from other areas of the church. Instead, missional communities seek an integrated structure that allows the missional purpose of the church to inform every area of church life. Some churches have adopted a new structure—the missional leadership team—to accomplish this purpose.

Usually, the missional leadership team comprises church members and leadership already involved in the church's missional task. This team is not designed to add more complexity to the church, but to bring together missional leadership that already exists. The team's task is to ensure that the church actively and appropriately involves its members and invests its resources in pursuit of God's mission. There is no right way for the structure to look. Gone are the days when a denominational entity or parachurch group could expect churches to adopt a uniform, one-size-fits-all structure. Yet the purpose of the missional leadership team is critical to every missional church. Each needs to:

- Discover and follow God's missional vision
- Equip members as authentic disciples
- Manage ongoing mission ministries effectively
- Involve people in new mission and ministries as God leads

The missional leadership team oversees the accomplishment of these needs and others as it fulfills its tasks. The team exists to:

- Pray for the church and its member involvement in God's mission
- Review and share with the congregation the activity of God through mission ministries
- Ensure adequate preparation for mission trips and ministries
- Identify new mission opportunities in which the church might participate
- Make sure that members are being equipped and invited to use their spiritual gifts in ministry (connect members with opportunities)
- Accumulate and compile annual budget requests for mission ministries
- Lead in developing emphases designed to educate and invite members' involvement in God's mission

The missional leadership team is made up of church members and leadership already involved in the church's missional task. The team should include:

- Leaders from existing ongoing ministries
- Mission education leaders
- Those involved in planning annual or other mission trips
- Discipleship training or other equipping personnel
- A deacon or other well-respected servant leader
- An individual involved in worship planning
- A representative of the church financial management and budgeting process

The team brings together representatives of all areas of church life who seek to ensure that the church's involvement in mission is not an isolated segment of church life, but an integrated purpose that informs every area. It is a flexible structure that adds representatives as the church identifies and initiates new mission ministries involving members in God's mission. Composition of the team differs with the church.

Preparing Members for Missional Tasks

Whatever format they may choose, missional churches develop structures that allow their members to live as authentic disciples who are sent by Christ into His mission. There are at least four areas to which this structure gives attention in preparing missional disciples.

Mission Education

Mission education includes exposing disciples to both the missionary passion of God and His activity in the world. Without the exposure to the missionary passion of God, members may learn about opportunities and ongoing mission ministry but lack the heart of God, which moves that knowledge to action.

Exposure to the missionary passion of God means the church consistently presents and interprets God as the premier missionary. The mission belongs to God rather than to His church. Bible studies, sermons, and other teaching ministries regularly highlight the heart of God longing that all people, all nations worship Him. Salvation history, the act of redemption, is interpreted in its missionary nature. Incarnation is understood as the primary mission function in history. God coming to man in the person of Christ serves as the model pursued by the church as followers are sent by Him to those who as yet are unreached. There will be no passion for missions until disciples touch the heart of God and are touched by Him.

Mission education also focuses disciples on the world in which they live and God's activity in that world. The church becomes a place where local needs, world geography, current events, and social conditions are constantly reviewed and discussed. These topics inform disciples as they reflect God's heart in their prayers. Members learn of nations where people experience oppression and injustice, where expression of faith is restricted, where poverty holds them in bondage, and where the Gospel has not reached.

They also learn what God is doing to transform communities and nations through the power of the Gospel. They link knowledge of the nations with awareness of the progress of God's mission in those places. They are moved to adopt unreached people groups as the focus of prayer and mission action. They pray for those who are serving the cause of Christ around the world. They learn of short-term opportunities through which disciples can be involved in God's mission purposes. They pray for liberation of oppressed peoples, for destruction or transformation of governments and regimes that restrict individual freedoms, and for national leaders who are standing for righteousness. They pray that all the nations will worship the missionary God. Prayer is specific rather than general because the nations have become so familiar to the disciple.

Mission education continues to include awareness of missionaries serving the cause of God's Kingdom throughout the world. It enhances this function to a personal and current reality. Church members receive regular e-mail updates from missionaries. They communicate their support for those missionaries in personal ways as well as through cooperative support. The news on print and broadcast media provides current information to update prayer concerns. In other words, mission education results in missional Christians being connected to the world, not just to the place they call home.

Mission Enlistment

Mission enlistment follows naturally from mission education. Once disciples have learned of Kingdom needs, activities of God in places where those needs exist, and viable means through which they might be involved in God's missional purpose, the desire for involvement is natural. Church structures must enable disciples to identify their personal make-up, how God has created them (including spiritual gifts, life experiences, and driving passions). Enlistment includes commitment to the everyday workplace, neighborhood, schools, and settings beyond.

Missional churches resist the tendency to communicate missions as activities that take place only somewhere else. They understand that the primary mission field for many disciples is the workplace, or school, or neighborhood where they spend most of their time. Enlistment invites every believer to surrender as God sends him or her on mission. As long as the realm of missions is perceived as being somewhere else, the sending of missionaries is limited to only select disciples, or to only brief experiences when disciples intentionally go beyond their everyday world. In fact, all are called into relationship with God, and all are sent as His emissaries, ambassadors, and missionaries. Sending is more relational than geographical.

Education concerning unreached groups, the activity of God, and mission opportunities result in disciples longing to be involved in missions beyond their own locale. Missional churches constantly present opportunities in which members can express their response to God's passion that all people have an opportunity to know Him. This might include short-term group mission trips, or long-term individual ministry opportunities. It might include weekend projects in the local community, weeklong commitments in a neighboring city or state, or extended partnership projects with believers in other nations.

Disciples cannot respond to opportunities about which they are uninformed, so the missional church keeps a variety of opportunities in front of its members. Through bulletin boards, e-mail communications, public announcements, and among various groups within the church who adopt particular mission projects, options for involvement are communicated regularly. Mission enlistment is designed to make it easy for disciples to commit their involvement in the purposes of God's Kingdom, beginning at home and extending to the ends of the earth. Enlistment leads the church to help reduce barriers that prohibit or restrict member involvement. For example, enlistment might ensure that those who sense God sending them to participate in a particular mission opportunity are assisted in raising needed funds for the ministry, or care for their children while the member is away.

Car dealers constantly advertise that there is "no excuse" for not purchasing a new or used vehicle (No credit? no problem! Financing available on the spot! All trade-ins accepted!). Mission enlistment seeks to remove any barriers that could prevent disciples from following the direction of God.

Mission Equipping

"Wanting to" and "knowing how" are not synonymous. Mission equipping is the missional church accepting responsibility for enabling disciples to move from wanting to, to knowing how. Although it is an everyday task of discipleship, equipping becomes situation-specific in the missional church. Since the first mission field for most disciples is the workplace, mission equipping is designed to prepare members to live as authentic disciples, serving and sharing in their workplace. Equipping provisions include contextual nuances for various settings—schools, factories, malls, restaurants. Equipping requires special instruction regarding legal requirements, and what an employee can and cannot do in a given environment. The church must not only equip people for the tasks they fulfill in the church, but also equip them for mission in the places where they live, work, and play.

Beyond the everyday workplace, members must be equipped for short-term and long-term opportunities to which they respond. In most instances, disciples responding to long-term commitments in cooperation with a mission agency are given cross-cultural and relevant context equipping by that agency. Members responding to short-term mission opportunities expect their church to provide the basic equipping needed to allow effective ministry to occur. At a minimum, this would include introduction to the national or people group lifestyle, cultures, habits, religious beliefs, and any needed health precautions. It might entail provision by the church of "survival instruction" in the languages of the nation or people group to which mission groups are being sent.

Mission Empowerment

Disciples experience no greater joy than serving as those equipped for ministry in the places of God's sending. Mission empowerment is the church releasing members to their own God-given ministry role. Where a church does not exhibit a missional culture, other church members may resent those who leave the local community, even for a short time, to minister in other places. Sadly, one might hear statements such as "We have so many needs right here at home, I just don't understand why we go spending money to send our people half way around the world." It is an attitude that restricts rather than releases. It fails to rejoice in God's sending of His servants in His Kingdom's mission.

The missional church empowers disciples for service by commissioning those who have been equipped as God's missionaries and representatives of their own local church. The empowering church regularly affirms those God is sending from the congregation to serve in other locations, just as it commissions its members as missionaries in their everyday workplace. In this church it is as normal to hear prayer offered for local church member "John Smith, our missionary to XYZ Utilities" as it is to hear prayer for "Dave Jackson, our missionary in Senegal."

In fact, the missional church understands that prayer empowers. The church is a prayer-based church. Prayer is essential to their plan for ministry and mission. Mission is the essence of the church, and prayer is an essential dialogue through which the church learns God's missional direction. Beyond affirming, commissioning, and praying for those sent by God, the missional church empowers members as it regularly hears the stories they share of God's activity in their mission endeavors. Bible study classes or business conferences are enriched as members hear reports from fellow members involved in the real business of the church: missions. Testimonies are included in times of worship and praise. PowerPoint or video presentations invite the entire Body to visually experience missions into which members have been sent. Praise songs of other nations find their way into the worship experiences of the missional church. Live telephone interviews are conducted during worship services, allowing members to hear "real-time" accounts of the activity of God among His extended family.

Mission empowerment is an attitude that manifests itself in actions that anticipate the blessings of God upon His church as His disciples walk obediently as those sent by Him. Missional churches that empower members for ministry invest richly and are rewarded abundantly. Such churches have a magnetic personality among believers who long for the depth of an intimate daily walk with the missional God of the ages.

Facilitating Structures

Missional congregations often develop additional structures to facilitate their missional purpose. *Key church* is one such structure that has been adopted by churches in various denominations. Key churches employ or enlist a "minister of missions," a church staff member whose role ensures missions are kept at the forefront of the church's passion, prayer, support, and involvement. Some ministers of missions serve as vocational staff while many are volunteer staff members. The key church process is both a missional structure and a mission strategy. Key church is a mobilization strategy designed to involve all church members in mission and ministry causes. Built on a foundation of prayer and evangelism, the key church strategy focuses the church's missions commitment in four areas:

1. Informative missions education for all age levels
2. Transformation of the church's local community through ministries
3. Involvement of members in short-term mission projects, locally, nationally, and globally
4. Starting new churches

The minister of missions looks beyond the church to identify mission needs and opportunities to which the church might respond, and into the church to discover members whom God might send to accomplish those ministries. Because new ministries require missionaries, the minister of missions is also involved in the ongoing development and equipping of church members for missions.

Beyond the local church, networking structures are assisting missional congregations in fulfilling their missional purpose. In some instances, these networks have been initiated by denominations or mission agencies at the request of churches. The Christian Missions Network is a ministry of Serving in Missions (SIM), an interdenominational mission-sending organization, but it serves all Christian missions. Generally, networks do not develop mission strategies for geographical areas; nor do they employ and send missionaries. Networks serve as cataloguing entities through which churches can learn of other Christian organizations with whom they share areas of focus and with whom they may partner in accomplishing similar visions for ministry and mission.

Antioch Community Church's strong commitment to church planting is enriched through their participation with Antioch Network (they share the name but are not otherwise affiliated). Antioch Network is a fellowship of churches sharing a common vision of sending church-planting teams to unreached people groups. It was born in 1987 as an informal meeting of leaders from seven churches around the United States, each of which was committed to church starting among unreached people groups. The network comprises churches of various traditions and theological perspectives, some affiliated with denominations and others independent. Developed around shared passions, the network allows the benefits of cooperative affiliation without compromising autonomy or requiring agreement on theological or ecclesiological issues. Networks permit flexible structures through which churches can be involved in the mission roles to which they sense God directing them. The singular focus allows networks to develop expertise in areas of specialization, thus becoming excellent resources to the Body of Christ as it serves the multifaceted initiatives of global missions.

Next-Generation Structural Expectations

Because every member is a missionary, the local church increasingly reclaims its role as the primary missions equipping center. Seminaries remain the principal equipping institution for people preparing to minister in academic environments, as well as for conventional church staff members. More second-career missionaries, the increase of business people accepting international positions in order to facilitate their involvement in Kingdom ministry, and young adults electing to serve in extended missionary service before settling vocational career objectives require churches to be the primary training center for missions. Whether in missions abroad or at home, churches must prepare their members for ministry in the marketplace. Offering the course "Perspectives on the World Christian Movement" is one example of how local churches are deepening their missional equipping. Meeting for fifteen to sixteen weeks, this intensive course introduces participants to the breadth of God's global activity in reaching the nations with the Gospel. Usually attended by disciples from various theological and denominational backgrounds, "Perspectives" challenges participants to focus on the essentials of the Gospel. Using lecture, extensive readings, interactive dialogues, and multimedia, "Perspectives" is being used to change supportive mission spectators into active participants in global missions. Sponsored by the U.S. Center for World Mission, this is the foundational course among others available to equip and educate disciples on the global frontier mission movement.

Beyond equipping, in next-generation structures local churches develop processes for sending and supporting their young adults in short-term missionary roles. Often considered a historic function of denominational agencies, increasingly churches are enabling their young adult members' service in extended-term global mission projects (often six months to two years). Greater global awareness, the ease and low cost of travel, and immediacy of communication technologies remove many barriers that previously prevented local churches from viewing themselves as capable of sending their maturing youth as missionaries. Where they formerly deferred to mission-sending agencies, local churches are increasingly accepting their role as the "sender," while viewing external agencies as resources available to assist them as needed. In the future, many who serve Kingdom causes around the world will be trained and sent from a local church context. Structures designed to accommodate this phenomenon will become commonplace in local churches.

A final structural transformation is already occurring but will increase in the future. Because missional communities act on values and priorities reflecting God's heart, the role of visionary apostolic leaders is enhanced. Missional leaders possess multiple skills and spiritual gifts. They establish leadership teams who share their vision and develop missional communities. The significant role of such leadership teams and those who make up community results in adapting decision-making structures. Instead of the conventional church paradigm in which elected church officers and committee members make directional decisions within their segment of ministry life, a more integrated process involves the entire missional community in challenging and complementing the directional paths articulated by visionary leaders. The structure is less procedure-oriented and more relational in nature. Some will argue the format is less efficient, but it proves more effective and inclusive in guiding the missional community toward God's purpose in the cultural white waters of dynamic change.

Reflection and Application

1. Reflect on your church structures. Assess the impact those structures have upon contemporary mission accomplishment. Give evidence of flexibility of church structures to accommodate ministry in the midst of change.

2. Before enlisting people to fill positions of leadership in organizations and committees, evaluate each task. Are positions that disciples are asked to fill significant, and needed? Do they contribute to the church's accomplishment of its mission? Consider "organized abandonment."

3. Propose revised structures to ensure effective missions education, enlistment, equipping, and empowerment of members for involvement in God's mission.

4. Consider similar settings in which church members are employed. Prepare and offer an equipping forum designed especially for one such setting (for instance, "Being on Mission as a Public Educator"). Incorporate required sensitivity to issues of faith in the marketplace specific to each segment.

5. Obtain information on a "Perspectives" course in your area. If none exists, offer to serve as the host facility for a new course. Seek to involve 50 percent of young adults in the course over the next five years. For information, contact the Perspective Study Program at www.perspectives.org, by phone at (626) 398-2125, or via mail at Perspectives Study Program, 1605 E. Elizabeth St., Pasadena, CA 91104–2721.

SUGGESTED READING

Dudley, C. S., and Ammerman, N. T. *Congregations in Transition: A Guide for Analyzing, Assessing, and Adapting in Changing Communities.* San Francisco: Jossey-Bass, 2002.

Getz, G. *Elders and Leaders: God's Plan for Leading the Church.* Chicago: Moody, 2003.

SEEING BEYOND THE HORIZON

THE NATURE AND TASK OF MISSIONAL LEADERSHIP

---

*So he shepherded them according to the integrity
of his heart, And guided them with skillful hands.*

—Psalm 78:72

*The mantle of leadership is bestowed on you by those
who grasp your mission and choose to follow you.*

—C. Gene Wilkes, *Jesus on Leadership*

DAWSON TROTTMAN, founder of the Navigators, once described travel across west Texas as "miles and miles *of* miles and miles." Standing on the plains, anyone who looks can see to the horizon. Fewer people, however, can see beyond the horizon. Missional leaders have such penetrating vision. As Robert Kennedy said, "Some men see things as they are and ask, 'Why?' Others see things as they could be, and ask 'Why not?'" Missional leaders see beyond the horizon to the heart of God; they are navigating their way into the future with the heart of God as their destination.

When asked what made him a great player, hockey legend Wayne Gretzky replied, "Most people skate to where the puck is. . . . I skate to where the puck is going to be." Missional leaders understand the implications of this statement. Peter Drucker is perhaps the most respected twentieth-century student of leadership; he wrote, "The future cannot be known and it will be different from what exists and what we expect it to be."[1] Missional leaders recognize the signs of impending change in today's reality, and they prepare to be there when tomorrow arrives. As Erwin McManus said, "My goal is not to keep up with the changing world, but to be standing there waiting for it when it arrives. People are going to need someone to show them the way."[2]

When God sought a leader, he looked for "a man after His own heart" (1 Samuel 13:14; Acts 13:22). If a congregation is to be shaped by God's heart, its leader must likewise be one after God's own heart.

Thus leadership is first about *being*: He shepherded them according to the integrity of heart. That is character.

Leadership is also about *doing*: He guided them with skillful hands. That is proficiency.

Leadership, then, is a composite of character and proficiency. Character has much to do with the inner person and little to do with capabilities or skill sets. Only when the personal issues of character and integrity are strong do skills and performance capabilities matter. Missional congregations are not established apart from leaders who possess these personal and performance criteria. Leadership may not be everything, but missional churches do not exist without visionary missional leaders.

Leaders must bring the personal criteria of heart integrity to the leadership challenge. Too frequently, people are called as leaders whose charisma and acumen outpace their personal integrity and character. This is a proven formula for meteoric rise and tragic downfall. When God chooses a leader for His missional people, His measure looks first into the heart.

As you observe church leaders whose congregations are remaining afloat and making progress in the journey toward being missional communities, you will notice a number of common characteristics. Not every leader gives evidence of all these traits equally, of course, but a clear pattern does emerge among these leaders. If you are striving to reframe your church as missional, it pays to review these traits and reflect on how they shape a *missional* leader in particular.

A Deep Intimacy with God

The missional leader's intimacy with God is critical. The *missio dei* demands relationship with the God whose mission it is. Foremost, missional leaders are those who have come into personal relationship as followers of Jesus Christ. They are not content to know *about* God; they hunger to *know God*.

In the fashion of Psalm 42:1, their souls long for God "as the deer pants for the water brook." Soul hunger is not satiated with professional status or perceived ministry success. These leaders seek the Lord while He may be found. Their sense of mission derives from the nature of the relationship God desires with them. They understand they did not choose God, but rather He chose them—for relationship and mission. They seek to know the heart of God.

Such was Moses' relationship with God. He asked for the opportunity to see God's face and was allowed to know His dynamic, life-changing presence. The experience shaped not only Moses but the people whom He would lead. In the words of Reggie McNeal, "He captured the heartbeat of a God intent on creating a people who would join him in his redemptive efforts. This insight not only would shape Moses' heart but also would frame the subsequent understandings of God in Judaism and Christianity."[3] Intimacy with God results in leaders being refashioned into His likeness, recreated in His image. Their minds are consumed with the purposes of God and bringing Him glory.

Dale Jones, pastor of Sterlingwood Church in Houston, Texas, began a journey into intimacy with God when he was thirteen. "I knew God was calling me to Himself when I was a teenager," Jones said. In 1981, Jones sensed God desired to use him as a leader, and in 1984 he and his wife, Donna, took their children and left their home to plant a new church. "I felt revival coming and my heart and imagination were on fire," Jones confessed. "I was looking for some big 'Eureka!' moments, but what happened was Romans 12:2. God increasingly transformed us by renewing our minds. And as our minds were renewed and changed by the Holy Spirit, we decided to agree with Him that He was calling us to join Him in His kingdom building and community transformation."[4]

Many Christian leaders, of course, have sought to experience intimacy with God. Most—if not all—of us can identify with this longing. The classic account of Brother Lawrence, *The Practice of the Presence of God*, reflects this sentiment: "Before we can love, we must know. We must know someone before we can love him. How shall we keep our 'first love' for the Lord? By constantly knowing Him better! Then how shall we know the Lord? We must often turn to Him, think of Him, behold Him. Then our heart will be found with our treasure."[5]

Personal Humility

Leaders who know God intimately exhibit profound humility. Carol Davis, executive director of Global Spectrum ministries, may have working relationships with more emerging missional leaders than any other mission executive in America. In our interview, she observed, "The one thing I have seen about [missional leaders] is they are very humble people and strong leaders, but they are not calling attention to themselves." In fact, says Carol, they often refer to their surprise at how God has blessed the churches they lead.

Perhaps a natural by-product of deep intimacy with God is personal awareness of our dependence upon Him. Dale Jones sensed God's invitation to participate in a city-reaching Kingdom initiative. "Even as my congregation pledged their support," he told me, "I grew increasingly fearful. Sure, I could believe that God wanted to transform our community. But did He want me to serve this vision? Surely He wanted someone younger, better, brighter. Increasingly, I wanted to run away."

This reaction is common among missional leaders. It is not a false humility, but a sincere awe that God would choose to use them. Missional leaders often identify with Moses ("Who am I, that I should go to Pharaoh . . . ?"). As often as they borrow Moses' sentiment, they hear the same response God spoke to Moses: "I will be with you . . . I have sent you" (Exodus 3:11–12).

It is the same sense portrayed in Deuteronomy 7:6–9: "The Lord did not set His love on you nor choose you because you were more in number than any of the peoples, for you were the fewest of all peoples, but because the Lord loved you."

The Experience of Deep Pain

A. W. Tozer believed God seldom used people greatly until He first allowed them to be hurt deeply. "Those Christian leaders who shook the world were one and all men of sorrows whose witness to mankind welled out of heavy hearts," says Tozer. "There is no power in tears per se, but tears and power ever lie close together in the Church of the First-born."[6] Missional leaders are no different.

Like many people, missional leaders may have also experienced deep personal pain that appears inexplicable as it is being experienced—the early loss of a parent, the later loss of a child, a great betrayal by one loved. Although deeply wounded, somewhere along the journey they begin to see the purpose in the pain. In their "dark night of the soul," they grow in dependence upon and relationship with God.

Sometimes the pain is the feeling of intense separation from the congregation, or even complete rejection. Moses experienced alienation among his own people, and the devastation later had a great impact. Reggie McNeal says, "His constant sense of being an alien among those he lived with and served had carved out in his heart a huge place for God to inhabit. Maybe this deficiency established in Moses a heart hunger to establish community with God. God frequently targets the dark places, the holes in the leader's heart. When God works through deficiencies, he frequently increases the leader's awareness of dependency on him."[7] One missional leader I spoke to remembered how frequently he found himself the recipient of derision among his pastoral peers and judicatory staff before his growing church gained notoriety. Now, he says, shaking his head, he is the "darling" of the conference platform.

Visionary leadership can be lonely, and some pain stems from the "holes in the leader's heart." Other pain results as leaders see what is not, as though it were. As the leader communicates a sense of direction, some challenge the leader's vision because it threatens their comfort with the status quo. Missional leaders learn to accept the pain of this rejection as a price of leadership.

A positive response from peers and congregants might bring momentary affirmation, but it cannot bring lasting joy. Missional leaders walk in the path of another who, upon watching significant numbers of his congregation decide to abort following his leadership, turned to his core group and said, "You do not want to go away also, do you?" (John 6:67). Missional leaders do not seek pain, but neither are they deterred when it is experienced.

The Ability to Take Risks

We all have dreams, but not everyone has the confidence necessary to risk in pursuit of the dream. Missional leaders are risk takers. This characteristic does not imply that missional leaders do not consider potential consequences of their actions. They do consider those consequences, but they also consider the risks associated with *not* taking action.

Missional leaders weigh the risks and determine the course of action they perceive to be on the heart of God. They are settled in their commitment to pursue His vision. Commitment results in a dangerous faith that risks everything to pursue God's mission. Like Daniel's refusal to bow in worship to Nebuchadnezzar's golden image, these leaders possess a faith that flies in the face of fear. "He will deliver us out of your hand, O king. But even if He does not . . . we are not going to serve your gods or worship the golden image" (Daniel 3:17–18).

Fellowship Bible Church, which covered an entire city block, was a church that most would deem tremendously successful. Yet missional leader Robert Lewis was not satisfied that the ministry was accomplishing

God's purpose. Lewis sensed God's vision that Fellowship Bible Church was not to continue spending its resources on itself, building facilities, but rather to become a church of irresistible influence investing resources in caring for people in its own community and beyond. He shared that vision with his affluent congregation. As he began to lead toward a new vision, some were unable or unwilling to affirm that direction. Though he cared about them and listened to their concerns, Lewis remained true to his sense of God's direction. Fellowship Bible Church began to change accordingly.

Risking all to follow Him ensures that His followers will experience discomfort. Sometimes, in moving toward God's preferred future, leaders risk losing some in whose lives they have invested. Missional leaders do not long for such an experience, but they do not let risk and pain deter their pursuit of the mission. In their hearts, missional leaders understand that if leaders are unwilling to accept risks, their lives are constricted from seeing possibilities beyond themselves and their own capacities. Hope fades, passion dims. With such an alternative in mind, they are willing to take the leap.

Being Uncomfortable with Comfort

All churches have three choices they can make with regard to their future function:

1. They can continue doing the same things.
2. They can do the same things better.
3. They can choose a new direction and do something different.

Many churches are content to continue doing the same things, especially if they are doing them well and they have grown comfortable. We say, "That's just the way we do things around here." When someone suggests that a change might be in order, we resist. The longing for comfort is powerful, and as a result the commitment of these churches is not to break new ground but to maintain what has been. Over a period of time, however, churches that continue doing the same things, maintaining the same organizational structures, keeping the same ministries, using the same methods for reaching new members, find themselves needing new resources. Missional leaders are not content to be ministers of maintenance. In fact, when things get comfortable, these leaders tend to be uncomfortable. In such a circumstance, they choose to take their church in a new direction. Even though their choice may hold the greatest prospect for transformational renewal of the maintenance-minded church, only infrequently do maintenance churches follow such leadership because it calls for moving beyond comfort, for letting go of control.

Missional leaders in traditional churches are brokers of deep change. They hold a vision for what the church might become: a different kind of church. They propose new ways of acting, challenging members to become God's missional people. They raise the bar on expectation of members. The reason their actions are so disconcerting for many is expressed by Robert Quinn, author of *Deep Change*: "Deep change differs from incremental change in that it requires new ways of thinking and behaving. It is change that is major in scope, discontinuous with the past and generally irreversible. The deep change effort distorts existing patterns of action and involves taking risks. Deep change means surrendering control."[8]

Missional leaders acknowledge they were never really in control. More, they are grateful to assert that control belongs to God alone.

Creative and Noncomforming

Missional leaders can be nonconforming. They tend to be highly creative and do not readily adopt limitations imposed by others. Such outside-the-box thinking leads missional leaders to consider more relevant ways of communicating the redemptive message in contemporary culture. They value the past, embrace the present, and focus on the future.

At Mosaic, in Los Angeles, missional leader Erwin McManus has encouraged expressions of creativity as a core value. As McManus told me, "We have a really high view of human creativity. We do not see a conflict between glorifying God and maximizing human capacity."[9] Periodically, Mosaic hosts a forum called Velocity that sometimes shocks those who have a traditional concept of church. As McManus describes it, "[Velocity] is an explosion of creativity. It's two hours of dance, drama, poetry, short film, and comedy all wrapped up in one experience. Recently a talent scout from Warner Brothers came to Velocity. After the event he graciously thanked me for creating an environment for emerging talent to develop. In the conversation he expressed his surprise that a church would allow this kind of experience."[10]

Missional leaders perceive purpose as more important than propriety. When faced with challenges, they develop new solutions rather than simply seeking solutions that have proven useful to others. They might, for example, start a new church in an urban club, meeting in a room that moments before was a dark, smoke-filled haven for alcohol and exotic dancers. They pick and choose elements of worship, mixing elements from liturgical and nonliturgical traditions. More often than not, they know people from the communities they are seeking to affect.

By caring more about accomplishing the mission than preserving the past, the missional leader's creativity can seem threatening to some church leaders. Outside-the-box thinkers may see the resources of the past not as something to be preserved but as the most fertile compost in which to grow something new.

Many Interests and Areas of Expertise

Missional leaders are inquisitive people with a great diversity of interests and expertise. They tend to have high proficiency in areas of interest unrelated to ministry, and they naturally form relationships with people from various professions and disciplines. Most could turn to other professions without difficulty, should the door of pastoral ministry be closed. I met missional leaders who enjoyed an array of activities unrelated to ministry: home construction, firefighting, computer technologies, travel consulting, nation building, motorcycle repair, and classic automobile restoration. In some instances, these were skills or interests the individuals developed prior to their commitment to ministry. Most leaders continue to dabble, learn, and enhance skills in areas unrelated to ministry.

This characteristic doubtless reflects continued learning as a priority for missional leaders. They not only benefit from the energy they gain by participation in the avocation of those pursuits and the mental discipline of learning; they also provide opportunities for relationships with individuals that would otherwise not be available. Wide-ranging areas of interest promote broader spheres of relationship and influence. Wider spheres of influence equal enhanced mission opportunity.

Cultural Engineers

Engineers fashion new designs for functionality and service, whether in buildings or systems. Cultural engineers help to fashion the structures necessary for the church to serve God's mission effectively.

The designation "cultural engineer" has more to do with *doing* than with *being*. It addresses the development of structures and systems, organization within the organism for equipping and empowering missional Christians. The role of cultural engineer is linked to provision of sacred place: to become, to live a life of missional integrity.

At Grace Point Church, Jeff Harris has led the congregation to view themselves as a place where members can become. "We have lots of folk who belong before they come to believe," he said. "We emphasize that none of us have it all together. In Christ, we are in the process of becoming. We seek to create an environment where becoming, growing is normative."[11] One example of cultural engineering at Grace Point was the decision not to use the traditional term "deacon" for servant leaders in the church. The criteria for servant leaders are those accepted as biblical norms for deacons in traditional churches, but Grace Point found the term was perceived as a bureaucratic or political position of leadership. To change this perception, they call servant leaders "point persons." Harris said, "*Deacon* carried too much baggage. We wanted to tap into the servant leadership pulse resonating in our leaders rather than transforming them into those perceived as bureaucrats."

Cultural engineers do not reject tradition. Rather, they seek to adapt systems and structures for the greatest missional effectiveness in their contexts. They do not lead churches in new directions just for the sake of innovation. They respect tradition as what allows past to inform present. In words attributed to Yale University professor Jaraslov Jan Pelikan, "Tradition is the living faith of those now departed. Traditionalism is the dead faith of those now living." Missional leaders engineer the future, rather than dwell on the past.

Challenging the Status Quo

A significant number of missional church leaders formerly served traditional maintenance churches before they started the missional communities they now pastor. They recognized that the power of the status quo in the traditional church was so strong that it would perennially be a challenge to overcome and lead in new directions.

Bob Roberts planted NorthWood Church for the Communities in 1985. He recounts their challenge in resisting traditional patterns and paradigms of success: "Our people were like others; they wanted our church to grow. We had reached about five hundred in active membership by 1992. God then began asking me some really hard questions, like, 'What will ever be big enough for you?'" Through an ongoing dialogue with God and church leaders, NorthWood affirmed its role to be a different kind of church. They chose not to employ programs just because other churches do them. They began to ask, "What would our church look like if it were truly missionary? What would it look like if of our church it could be said, 'They have turned the world upside down'?" Such questions have radically affected their development.

Pastor Harris told me about the painful departure of founding members who had come from a traditional church to assist in starting up Grace Point Church. "When we made the decision not to assign the title [of] deacon to our servant leaders, we had a number of families who left. One said, 'I have never been in a church that did not have deacons. I am not going to now.'" Tragically, the member could not resolve the issue of the new term. The power of the status quo, the way we do things, was too strong. The member family returned to the traditional church from which they had come.

Status quo is not sacred to missional leaders. They value methods that are most effective in the context where mission is being expressed. They are not afraid to pursue a new paradigm. Martin Luther King Jr., was a historic challenger of the status quo. Leonard Sweet, author of *AquaChurch*, applied one of King's phrases—"divinely dissatisfied"—to churches: "Our churches need to be 'divinely dissatisfied' with the way things are and divinely driven to create some new realities."[12] When it comes to mission, missional leaders choose new realities over status quo. They are divinely driven.

Perceived as Radical in Pursuit of Their Vision

As missional leaders seek alignment between vision and values, they may engender conflict. When a leader acts courageously on convictions involving others, and with which they are not in agreement, the leader is likely to be labeled "radical."

Missional leaders are decisive individuals whose sense of God-directed vision motivates their actions. When they know where God wants His Body to move, they will not be deterred. Conflict can arise if parishioners are not equally certain that the leader's vision is God-directed, or if their commitment to obey His vision is not predetermined. If disciples have not given up control of their faith community to the purposes of God, conflict will result. Since a missional church is a reproducing community of authentic disciples being equipped as missionaries sent by God to live and proclaim His Kingdom in their world, one might assume the matter of instant obedience has been settled. However, missional leaders and those they shepherd still wrestle with total surrender to God's purpose.

If a missional congregation's vision and action path are not aligned, the leader seeks alignment. If members remain unwilling to submit their actions to what the leader perceives as the God-given vision, continued pursuit of the vision may result in their perception of the leader as being irrational or radical.

Mosaic's Erwin McManus sees this issue as a conflict between values and vision:

> I have an almost ruthless perspective of evaluating whether a person's actions can accomplish a vision. I cannot live with myself if they do not line up. I can change my vision to fit my value systems, or change the value systems to fit the vision, but I can't live with an articulation of one vision and a value system that can't get there. I'm just not built that way. And so there is that sense where I do tend to move people to a decision.
>
> I don't think I can change a person's value systems. I don't even think I am necessarily responsible to do that. But I do think that I'm responsible to make sure we're honest. And if we're going to say we're going to do something, then we have to be willing to pay the price to accomplish that, or we need to relinquish that vision and say, 'You know, that's not us.'[13]

Understanding, Constructing, and Altering Organizational Systems

Many leaders have wonderful ideas, deep conviction, and directional vision. Fewer have the capacity to carry a vision from concept to reality. Moving from the idea held by one person to a mutually held commitment of a group is one of the measures of missional leadership.

New Heights Church in Vancouver, Washington, is a missional community that has grown from about two hundred to more than four thousand worshippers under the leadership of Matt Hannan. As he described the challenges the congregation faced early in his leadership, Matt said, "There is a huge spiritual dimension. And when you talk about any church being turned aside, there is a mechanical component. It is mechanical and spiritual. My presentation of the church is as an organism and an organization. You have to attend to both realities or else you are going to fail."[14]

Under Hannan's leadership, New Heights has initiated many diverse ministries, including community medical clinics, programs of a twelve-step style, and support groups. Each of those ministries requires financial support from the church budget. Many schedule use of the church's facilities at various times. All merit the encouragement and prayer support of both church staff and fellow members. With about two dozen full-time and part-time staff members seeking to equip and deploy more than four thousand members, organization is mandatory.

Although the church is by definition more than an organization, it still requires leadership with the capacity to understand the larger system and the know-how to move the system forward in unity. Some missional leaders have obtained a postgraduate degree in organizational management. Others have a background in which they were actively involved in systems management. Still others provide excellent leadership without formal preparation or professional experience in organizational behavior.

Whether their expertise is learned or intuitive, missional leaders understand how change works in organizations. They are able to mobilize the qualities Malcolm Gladwell talks about in *The Tipping Point* functioning as connectors, mavens, or salesmen.[15] He describes *connectors* as people who have an instinctive, natural gift for making social connections. They know lots of people. *Mavens* are knowledge brokers; they know things others do not and want to share helpful information with others. *Salesmen,* on their own, would have never discovered the knowledge that mavens possess. But once they receive that knowledge from a maven, salespeople are passionate about sharing it with others and credibly communicate information to the benefit of the recipient.

Missional leaders—mavens one and all—are deeply committed to the vision they hold. They share that vision with others in the community who come to believe in the vision just as deeply as the leader. Some of them are salespeople. Passionate about sharing what they know with others, they do so with deep credibility. Ultimately, the vision is shared with connectors, those who possess an instinctive social gift for connecting with lots of people. In this process, the organizational system is able to make adaptations toward accomplishing the ultimate vision. This is certainly not the only means through which leaders facilitate systemic development and change, but it can help us understand why some leaders are much more effective in leading churches to accomplish mission than others.

Establishing Effective Leadership Teams

Missional leaders understand that they can't accomplish everything themselves. Those who have been drawn close to the heart of God are constantly reminded how dependent they are. In their humility, they readily recognize the need for a team around them, people who can fill in the gaps and address implications of the vision that might be overlooked by the leader alone.

Here is a tension of leadership. "Leadership" may assume a single leader, but it does not discount multiple leaders who each contribute their expertise and insight. When the space shuttle *Columbia* was tragically lost moments before it was to land, NASA personnel from various locations and centers responded to the loss personally. Whether from the launching site in Florida or at the Control Center in Texas, scientists and engineers, administrators and employees, each contributed certain important tools to the Columbia mission. Consequently, each sensed the loss as part of the team.

In fact, we can learn leadership lessons from corporate tragedies. Preceding the collapse of Enron, it is clear that at least one member of the leadership team fervently attempted to call attention to accounting practices that, if unchanged, threatened the company's ultimate destiny. Unfortunately, others in the leadership team discounted the warnings. Whether for selfish interest or from blindness, other leaders allowed practices to continue unchecked that resulted in the demise of the corporation they served.

The value of leadership teams cannot be overestimated. Some church members expect the senior pastor to exercise hands-on administration of every ministry their church offers. In larger churches with complex ministries, this is not only impractical, it restricts the effectiveness of the church in accomplishing its mission. Jimmy Seibert, pastor of Antioch Community Church, explained how he perceives his role: "I'm the visionary leader, but 95 percent of the pastoral care happens through the cells. Each of these areas is led by a visionary leader. They are visionary leaders who will eventually lead movements. They rally their own tribe, if you will, and then we rally together, which keeps creativity going on. This gives young visionaries an opportunity to continue to develop and not feel stifled in a larger system. So I'm becoming more of the senior leader than the senior pastor."[16]

Not only do leadership teams strengthen the corporate pursuit of mission, they also effectively develop new leaders. Leadership teams are strengthened as mature and novice leaders contribute alongside one another. The contribution of a variety of people in a leadership team results in a more flexible organization, one that is adept at change.

Developing Missional Communities

Missional leaders, along with their leadership teams, have a clear vision for creating authentic missional communities. Everything they do is designed to facilitate development of Christians as missionaries sent by God to live and proclaim His Kingdom in their world. Ultimately, the leadership team desires every member of the community to function in a missional lifestyle, equipped and empowered for effective ministry.

The missional church is a greenhouse where new leaders are constantly being cultivated. Leaders seek to be transparent and vulnerable among the community, modeling the kind of authenticity that is required for effective community to continue. Their language becomes inclusive—more "we" and less "I," more "our" and less "my." They understand that unless they model the practices and values they profess, authentic missional community will not happen.

Ultimately, such missional leaders are shaping the culture of their community. Their ultimate goal is that every member of the congregation experience intimacy with God and community with fellow believers while becoming leaders themselves. The measure of the leader is ultimately assessed in the nature of the community where leadership has been invested.

Max De Pree, after forty years as a CEO in corporate business, wrote: "The goal of thinking hard about leadership is not to produce great or charismatic or well-known leaders. . . . The signs of outstanding leadership appear primarily among the followers. Are the followers reaching their full potential? Are they learning? Serving? Do they achieve the required results? Do they change with grace? Manage conflict?"[17] The same can be said of missional leaders. They are validated when truly missional communities result from their leadership.

The Primary Task of Missional Leaders

Missional leaders possess dual vision. They see two worlds—present and future—with clarity.

Their view of current reality is honest. Like industrial safety inspectors, they point out potential hazards and note dangerous practices. The capacity to assess the present accurately is vital if churches are to be transformed from maintenance to missional. Missional leaders assess the current reality with accuracy and understand the destination toward which pursuit of that reality leads.

Their view of the future is also honest. They see the future that will result through continuation of practices that have resulted in the current reality. They also see a preferred future, a future that will result if the church is shaped by God's heart. This is the future that can come into being as it becomes a new kind of church, reshapes its practices to reflect a missional vision, and is transformed by the Spirit. This future is a compelling vision for the missional leader. As vision of the preferred future is sharpened, it becomes the motivator that shapes the direction of leadership.

For many church members, it's a whole new experience. To some, such observations can seem ruthless or painful. Many people see the world not as it is, but through a filter of their own perception. Those who have been part of the church for any significant time may be relatively comfortable with the way things are. They may be convinced that if the church just does better what it has done in the past, its future will be secure. Other church members may be more open to the possibility that realizing the preferred future might require making significant changes. They support leadership and are personally involved in pursuing new directions in order to reach the preferred future.

The primary task of the missional leader is to maintain creative tension between the current reality and the preferred future. Think of a large rubber band with a person on either end. As one stays in place, the other steps away, stretching the rubber band. With each step it is stretched tighter, toward its maximum capacity. As the tension increases, the two individuals begin to fear the consequence of continued stretching. As the person stepping further away takes another step, the person who has remained stationary might decide to take a step toward her partner in the exercise. She is seeking to eliminate further tension.

Let's say the person we have designated as not moving represents current reality, and the other person represents the preferred future. When current reality takes a step away from her position to prevent further tension, she is altering current reality. Movement from the current reality— saying reality is not as it is—is distortion. Those who have been a long time in a given culture might not agree with the assessment of their current reality. Churches make a grave error when they fail to assess their current state accurately. Distortion of current reality prevents us from making appropriate decisions concerning the future. We must know where we are to know which way to go.

In similar fashion, assume the person designated "preferred future" grows concerned about exceeding the rubber band tension quotient. The participant takes a step toward current reality and away from the position of preferred future. Diversion from the preferred future, failure to keep that future as the vision toward which the church invests its efforts, is compromise. When compromise is accepted, the preferred future is abandoned. Compromise is opting for action paths that, although posing less resistance in the short run, do not result in arrival at the desired destination. Compromise is the death of a vision.

Maintaining creative tension between current reality and future vision expends a high level of energy. Keeping the rubber band stretched to its limit over a long period of time is challenging. The situation longs for resolution. The leader knows that tension is most often reduced through compromise or abandonment of the preferred future.

Maintaining status quo is so comfortable. The authors of *Leading Congregational Change* put it succinctly: "Institutional hierarchies are designed for compliance, not for innovation."[18] For the missional leader, abandoning the preferred future to reduce tension is not an option. There is only one acceptable alternative. Ultimately, the leader knows tension lessens when the current reality begins to change and move toward the future vision. Genuine change of current reality toward the preferred future, no matter how minimal, is progress! Like a child's stumbling forays in learning to walk, small steps encourage the heart that full-blown movement is possible.

In maintaining tension between current reality and preferred future, missional leaders become artists painting word pictures that allow others to see God's preferred future. As members envision the preferred future, they ask, "Why must that future be ours?" The "why" is critical. It requires the church to revisit the very essence of its existence, its purpose or mission.

Once the question of *why* has been addressed and the congregation has clearly discerned its purpose, the church is ready to move forward in developing strategy. "What actions will lead us toward that purpose?" The missional leader's role demands carrying God's people through the "Why?" to the "What?" Once there, the leader must then be willing to risk failure as congregants articulate their understanding of *how* that purpose might be reached. High energy and creativity are in evidence when a congregation's members have a clear sense of purpose and are challenged to forge the pathways they will take in pursuing that direction. Leadership teams and missional communities thrive in the atmosphere of exploration, finding ways that lead to preferred future. Together, they are on mission.

The Leadership Question

Clearly, not every pastor possesses the traits or has the energy for maintaining creative tension. Too often, churches grow frustrated under their leader's constant pressure to become something other than what they are. Other congregations, longing for a more active missional role, are thwarted by leadership that desires only to maintain the existing organizational structures to the highest degree of effectiveness. Much consternation can be avoided if congregations and leaders identify their openness to change and change management in advance. Figure 13.1 presents a framework for discussing this issue.

Figure 13.1. Change and Change Management.

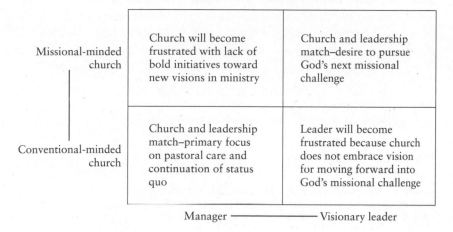

	Manager ———————————— Visionary leader
Missional-minded church	Church will become frustrated with lack of bold initiatives toward new visions in ministry	Church and leadership match–desire to pursue God's next missional challenge
Conventional-minded church	Church and leadership match–primary focus on pastoral care and continuation of status quo	Leader will become frustrated because church does not embrace vision for moving forward into God's missional challenge

Can leadership be taught, or is leadership an innate trait? Are leaders born, or are they made? Can a congregation longing for change call a manager and expect him or her to become a change leader? One must acknowledge that everybody is capable of growth and development. God's disciples live in the constant tension between "already" and "not yet." No one is eliminated from potential leadership. Our model has discussed leadership as a combination of personal makeup and proficiencies, of being and doing.

Proficiencies and skill sets can be learned and developed through practice. Techniques can be learned and applied. The more difficult challenge is in developing real missional leadership. Missional leaders must see what is *not* as though it *were*. The ability to see beyond the horizon and to "walk naked into the land of uncertainty" requires faith. Even the secular leadership literature frequently speaks of this intangible quality.

Those in Christian ministry understand faith as a spiritual issue. We experience the truth that all persons are created with the capacity to express faith. We know that "without faith, it is impossible to please God." Salvation is a grace gift from God afforded to those who confess faith in Him. Yet we discover some whose faith appears much deeper than for others. For every Abraham who would bind his only son to a makeshift altar, believing God would provide the sacrifice, we observe others whose faith, in the face of sacrifice or danger, does not measure well. We each experience the challenges that call our faith to deeper trust as we go kicking and screaming into experiences we would rather avoid.

Missional leaders are not always born, but they can be born again. They are those who have first experienced depth of relationship with God, intimacy that gives confidence in His ability and faithfulness to keep His promises. They grow to know Him intimately and trust Him completely as they lead His Body to relinquish every other ambition and live His mission.

Reflection and Application

1. Describe specifically how you can encourage your church's leaders to exemplify one of the characteristics of missional leaders discussed in this chapter.

2. Which leadership characteristics might be most threatening to your church? In your opinion, which are least visible among your church leaders?

3. Appraise the potential use of *foresight* rather than *vision*. Are the two synonymous? If not, what are leadership implications in identifying the preferred future on the basis of the former and the latter?

4. What do you "see" just beyond the horizon in the context of your church? Have others observed the same future prospects? How can your vision or foresight prepare the congregation for the future?

5. Support the statement, "Our minister was chosen on the basis of his or her missional vision."

6. Verify the congregation's acceptance of and benefit from the minister's missional vision.

SUGGESTED READING

Hamel, G., and Prahalad, C. K. *Competing for the Future*. Boston: Harvard Business Press, 1994.

Hasselgrave, D. J. *Scripture and Strategy: The Use of the Bible in Postmodern Church and Mission*. Pasadena, Calif.: William Carey Library, 1994.

McIntosh, G. L., and Edmondson, R. L. *It Only Hurts on Monday: Why Pastors Quit and What You Can Do About It*. Carol Stream, Ill.: ChurchSmart Resources, 1998.

Payne, Bishop C. E., and Beazley, H. *Reclaiming the Great Commission: A Practical Model for Transforming Denominations and Congregations*. San Francisco: Jossey-Bass, 2000.

14

MOVING TO MISSIONAL

BECOMING A NEW KIND OF CHURCH

Delight yourself in the Lord; And He
will give you the desires of your heart.

—Psalm 37:4

Whom God sends he employs, for he sends none to
be idle. What were candles made for but to burn?

—Matthew Henry

JERRY BARKER told the congregation he pastors, "Don't call me to be your pastor if you want things to stay the way they are." It was not a threat, nor meant to be rude. His calling is to help churches rediscover their reason to exist: God's mission. Becoming a new kind of church—moving to missional—is a deep change that is inherently difficult because it requires leaving established ways of doing things. Members who are comfortable in the conventional church, with its many programs and services designed primarily for members, will likely resist departure. But for those who have found something vital lacking in their church experience, embarkation is the beginning of an exciting new journey.

As with any journey, it helps to have at least some idea of where you are going. In this final chapter, we look at the issues involved with making this transition.

Where Is Your Church on the Mind-Set Continuum?

Moving an existing church to a missional mind-set is a momentous challenge because it means adapting the behavior of a group of people—one of the most difficult types of change. As change goes, behavioral scientists have observed that change in knowledge is the quickest and easiest to accomplish. Change in attitude is more difficult and requires more time. Change in action that is based upon new knowledge and attitude requires significantly more time and proves difficult. The highest challenge, in terms of both difficulty and time required, is group behavioral change. Of course, the closer your church is to wanting change, the easier it is. So determining how your church feels about change is an important first step.

As is the case in human life, congregations have a life cycle. They also have a corporate mind-set that may be related to where they are in the life cycle. Their mind-sets may be conventional, survival, terminal, or missional. Churches of each mind-set act differently from those in other mind-sets. Step one, then, is understanding where your congregation is on the mind-set continuum: conventional, survival, terminal, or missional?

Conventional Churches

Conventional churches often exhibit a maintenance orientation. Frequently found in growing communities, these churches are commonly building or planning new facilities to have adequate space for worship, education, fellowship, and ministry. In this environment, they often expend most of their resources on themselves. As members express desire for various services, conventional churches expand the number and kind of programs afforded their members.

Addition of programs is often accompanied by employment of new staff members to direct them. Usually the growing conventional church has a well-rounded representation of people of all ages. The energy and diversity of ministries offered members, and the excitement generated through establishment of new relationships, creates an energetic and winsome vitality to which new members are drawn. Many new members may have been part of congregations in communities where they lived previously; they attach to the new church through transfer of membership.

Rapid growth can challenge the church's capacity to effectively equip members, resulting potentially in developing members only superficially.

Conventional churches are typically committed to a missions program that challenges members to pray for and give financially to support missionaries serving globally. Relatively few members would identify themselves as missionaries in their own sphere of influence.

Survival Churches

As conventional congregations age and demographics change in their communities, these churches gradually move to a primary focus on survival. They become increasingly isolated from the community. Having spent years together, congregations become like family, caring for one another. Even though many members may have relocated from the area in which their church facility is located, they drive back into the community to remain part of the fellowship.

Distanced from residents around them, the church fails to continue reaching new people. One might observe the absence of an entire age segment (young families with children, for instance) in the church composition. The church finds itself hoping to reach at least as many people as it loses in any given year, enough to enable their continued care for facilities and vital programs. Although they may attempt sporadic initiatives with the hopeful outcome of growth (addition of a youth minister is routinely observed), these efforts rarely result in a significant influx of new members who are actually assimilated into the congregation.

Churches in a survival mind-set value continuity with the past in worship style, program initiatives, and ecclesial structures. Conversation is replete with references to a previous era; this church believes its best days are behind them. Creativity, if present, is kept on a leash. Fear often steals the place of faith regarding the future. Optimism gradually surrenders to despondency. Without intentional commitment to change, the survival-minded church's diagnosis at some point becomes terminal.

Terminal Churches

When a congregation does not have enough resources to cover the costs of ministry and it lacks ability to generate new sources of support, it is terminal. Barring a miraculous intervention, its demise is inevitable.

The terminal congregation is often a dim reflection of the church that once existed: a handful of older members, unlike others in the neighborhood, struggling to keep the doors open and the lights on in their place of worship. They are disconnected from the community. Not necessarily viewed negatively, they simply do not show up on the radar screen of those living around the church facilities. Members know that if the heating system goes out in winter, the cost of repairs might be enough to move them from being marginal to extinct.

Moving Each Mind-Set to Missional

Churches in the late-survival or terminal mind-set may be most open to potential change, especially when the fear of death becomes greater than the fear of change. Although a reflection of the survival instinct, openness to potential change also results from a spiritual desire to see a continued presence of the Kingdom operating in what has become a sacred place for them.

Openness to potential change does not mean such change can or will be made. Terminal congregations often lack the resources necessary to make significant change without receiving assistance from outside the congregation. Survival churches may be poised to make the radical changes required to become relevant, provided they are able to identify adequate resources. This kind of transition is still immensely difficult and potentially painful. In most instances, the majority of members are not able to make the journey. They can, however, bestow their blessings upon a leader and the minority membership who are committed to adopt a missional mind-set. In most instances, such transition is initiated at a juncture when some church members realize continuation of the same processes will only yield the same results. They know something must change.

Growing conventional churches might find the disturbance associated with the journey to missional a distraction. They often find it most difficult to embrace change because they are not in a crisis, have adequate resources, may be growing, and must first meet the program and ministry expectations of their members. Still, change is possible. The pastor and these leaders may experience a spiritual process of renewal in which they sense God's purpose in focusing beyond themselves in mission. They realize no programs are capable of correcting spiritual problems. This small group, seeking God's will, surrender themselves anew as His servants. In the experience, they find new hope and strength for the task. They begin to share Ezekiel's confidence that "these bones can live again." Like Abraham and Sarah, the time appears long past when new life could have been produced, yet laughter is promised to them. These believers become a small missional community within the larger Body.

Are *You* Ready to Move?

"Leader, know thyself" is an important axiom for those seeking to move a traditional church toward a missional expression. Fortunately, many instruments are available to help individuals gain insight into their personal preferences in a leadership situation.[1] Comparing your personal leadership preferences with the list of leadership traits found in Chapter Thirteen can be a framework for assessing the comfort with which you might lead through conflict and deep change. Remember, though, God has a unique way of using those who do not perceive themselves to be gifted for a task. If it is His will for you, He will lead through you.

Beginning the Transition

The transition process begins with a missional community who can envision change and who are willing to yield themselves to God's purpose. The pastor leader must champion the cause of these disciples in whose lives the future of the church lies. While championing them, the pastor must also continue to extend consistent and loving ministry to other members who are not able to share the future vision. The pastor must avoid caring for the developing missional group at the expense of those who cannot envision a new kind of church. Relationship with the latter group is critical, since they must give their blessing to the developing missional community.

As the missional cell is equipped to live missionally, they establish relationships with outsiders and begin to join them on the journey to knowing God. The missional community grows in number. Through continued exposure to God's Word, disciples' spiritual roots deepen in their relationship with God. Their commitment to live what they are learning results in lifestyles that attract people who have no relationship with God. Struggles in faithfulness will be acknowledged in the missional community with subsequent encouragement and support. Authenticity in relationships has transformational impact within the missional cell and in the community.

Potential Dangers

Associated with developing the missional community, a subset or cell within the church, there are at least two dangers that must be avoided. First, the missional community must shun the pretense of viewing themselves as "more spiritual" than members of the church who do not pursue the missional vision. The enemy seeks to destroy any fresh work of

God's Spirit; perhaps no tool is more pliable for that use than spiritual pride. Those who are experiencing spiritual growth must remain cautiously humble as they communicate the activity of God within their lives. If the missional cell is perceived as thinking of themselves as more spiritual, internal battles between segments of the church will soon destroy any advancement made in becoming a missional people.

A second danger can result as numeric growth takes place within the missional cell. This subset begins to increase in number, and what started out as a small group can soon become as large as the balance of the church's membership. In fact, a new kind of church is being planted within the existing church. Where those members not involved in the missional cell once gave their blessing, and in fact reacted with warmth as new members began to unite, now they may begin to resist the potential loss of control and power associated with a rapid influx of new members into the missional subset. This danger can be exacerbated as the missional community begins to invest more resources in mission causes beyond the local church.

Pastors and church leaders must create opportunities for ongoing dialogue between the missional subset and other members of the church. If dialogue continues and transition is most effective, people in the latter group begin to move toward the former as they vicariously experience fresh encounters of God in their midst. Where the initial few walked by faith, others follow as they see the blessing of God upon those committed to be His missional disciples.

Starting a Church

While considering becoming missional, some churches may determine to become that kind of church. But the most effective (and least painful) way to develop a missional church is to start one from scratch. Existing churches play an important role in developing new ones. In some instances, a new church can be born out of a missional cell begun as a part of an existing church. In this instance, the result can be one church with two diverse congregations. The same pastor might serve both congregations, one focusing primarily on pastoral care giving and the other on reaching and discipling new believers. Other existing churches, however, may decide their highest long-term impact results from birthing a new church start.

In such sponsoring roles, the existing congregations sometimes provide a few members to become the core around which the new church develops. Those individuals must be committed to developing a church that is different from their origin. They can serve as liaison to the sponsor church, ensuring appreciation is expressed and victories are shared with the sponsor. Some sponsor churches or judicatories assist in underwriting expenses as the new church is beginning. In many instances, the founding pastor and core group meet for a period of time before going public as a congregation. During this period the new church is developing relationships with unchurched persons who may become the church's first generation of new disciples.

How Jerry Barker's Church Moved to Missional

When you begin any new enterprise, it always helps to see how someone else did it. Let's look now at how one church made the transition to missional.

Jerry Barker is pastor of a one-hundred-year-old county seat First Baptist Church in South Texas. When he became pastor of the church five years ago, he came to a church clearly in the survival mode: a totally Anglo congregation in a community that was 95 percent Hispanic. The church held worship services and Bible Study in the same way they had been doing for years. They operated with the same program structures they had inherited from their grandparents. The primarily older adult congregation wanted their church to have a positive impact in their community, but lacked direction to accomplish that purpose.

Barker began to talk informally with a few members who longed to see the church connect missionally with those in its community. They discussed what they could do to become relevant to people who had never come into their church. The first thing they realized was that their facility itself was a resource. This building, virtually unused six days a week, was an asset they could share with the community. So they offered their facility to community service providers and gradually became home to Boy Scouts, the 4-H club, an aerobics class, a diabetic support group, a neighborhood crime watch group, and the Citizen's Police Academy. Even though church members were not leaders in any of those entities, by reaching out and being receptive the church gradually became known as the place where you can get help in the community.

The seed group also reached out to their fellows. Constant dialogue kept church members informed about what was going on in their facility. Members had to let go of feeling they should all be there every time the doors were opened, but some church members were always available. As more people came to the facilities for community events, they gradually began to develop relationships with some church members. Some started to attend worship at the members' invitation.

The church began to release its sense of doing things from obligation and started to adapt its activities to better serve its members and community. They discontinued Sunday and Wednesday evening services, giving greater focus to the Sunday morning experience. Members chose to move worship from the formal sanctuary into a more informal fellowship area of their building.

They risked trying new forms. They chose to jettison the Bible Study curriculum they had used year after year, replacing it with studies of contemporary publications such as the *Prayer of Jabez* and *Seekers of the Vine*. If something did not work, they agreed to consider the failure as a step to success: "That didn't work, so let's try something else."

Over the past two years, the church has made significant change—and it's not over yet. Today, First Baptist is experiencing new vitality, which members express as "renewal" or "revival." They are once again making a difference in the lives of those in their community. The difference is not just relational or social, but spiritual. Barker's church has decided to call themselves "the missional people of God." They have reclaimed the missional purpose for which they exist. In their words, "We did not change the reason we do things, just the way we do them."

This is an inspiring and encouraging story, and it also offers some concrete action steps you can consider in your own move to missional:

- They compared the church population with that of the community to assess its effectiveness in penetrating its mission field.

- They acknowledged both their desire to connect with the community and their seeming inability to do so.

- They made a decision to offer their resources to community service providers, beyond their own ability.

- They kept communication going with other church members and dealt with internal issues as they arose.

- They celebrated the arrival of new faces into the church facilities, establishing relationships with many of those people.

- They practiced organized abandonment in releasing forms and structures whose continuance was done from a sense of obligation.

- They encouraged "what if we . . ." discussions and incorporated new ways of being church into their practices.

- They accepted any failure as a step toward success, and kept trying.

Today, Barker's church has new faces in worship. Older members voted to continue worshipping in the informal fellowship area, seated at round tables. They now enjoy coffee during worship services. This might seem a small thing to some, but it represents a world of change in what was a traditional survival-oriented church. They are again reaching people in their own community. They are again on mission.

Taking Your Own Steps Toward Missional

As a leader, you must understand your congregation's readiness to embrace the changes required to become a missional community. Prerequisite to any change strategy is an understanding of where your church is on the spectrum from terminal to missional. You can assess your point on that continuum by amalgamating church historical data, community demographics, and perceived ministry opportunities together with current church membership analysis in a filtering process. In the process, you will ask questions of this kind: How closely does our congregation match our community? Are entire age segments absent within our congregational constituency? Do we have the adequate resources, energy, and will to begin new ministries?

Assessing your church's readiness to move and then moving is not a small thing; I have written entire how-to guides for churches on this process, and this book is not the place for such detail. Still, I would like to leave you with several points to consider as you seek to refocus toward a missional mind-set.

Study Your Congregational History

Even if you have been a member of your church for years, you may not have a realistic picture of its current state. These tools can help sharpen your understanding.

IS YOUR CHURCH MISSIONAL-MINDED? Complete the Missional Church Cultural Assessment in the Appendix. This is a quick and effective way to see where your church currently stands on each of the missional practices discussed in this book.

HAS YOUR CHURCH GROWN OR DECLINED? Prepare a profile of church growth or decline over the most recent decade. Include graphs or tables:

- Enrollment and participation in Bible Study organization
- Congregational participants by age groups
- New members or communicants added during the last three years

- Members or communicants lost during the same period
- Net growth or decline by year
- Financial receipts
- Percentage of budget annually dedicated to mission causes

Church leaders and members can then study this profile for a real-time picture of your church's growth—or lack of growth—in recent years.

WHERE DO MEMBERS LIVE? Make a pin map depicting the location of where members live. This map should include a dot for every active member of the congregation:

- Green dot to indicate membership for three years or less.
- Yellow dot to indicate membership for three to seven years.
- Red dot to indicate membership for more than seven years.
- Some choose to add a black dot to indicate inactive members.

It is critical that your map reveal where new members are being reached. Generally, a congregation will most effectively reach additional new people in areas from which most recent additions have come. If those areas are some distance from your church facility, you might encourage newer members to begin inductive Bible studies in their homes for persons in their neighborhood.

Study Your Community

Your church should not be an island in the community. Before you begin to reach out, begin with a good idea of who your neighbors are.

WHO LIVES HERE? The easiest way to find out who lives in your community is to look at demographic profiles indicating population and change trends. You can obtain this information from various governmental offices, among them the U.S. Census Bureau, local or county governments, your town's Chamber of Commerce, denominational or judicatory offices, or from private firms such as Percept (see www.percept.info.com).

WHAT DOES YOUR COMMUNITY NEED? Conduct a community needs assessment with service providers in schools, health care, human services, police departments, and other social agencies. For helpful instructions, contact Missions Equipping Center, 333 North Washington, Dallas TX 75246.

DO YOU KNOW YOUR NEIGHBORS? Encourage members to create a "members inventory" of those they know within the proximity of the church facility who have no relationship with a church. Survival or terminal churches often realize they cannot actually name those who live around the church facility and have no faith connection. In many instances, members drive into the neighborhood where their church facility is located only to attend church events. They may have no other connection with the immediate area. If this is the case, the church must determine how to connect with those in the community.

Strategic Vision Plan

Once you are armed with real information, you can develop a strategic vision plan for becoming a missional church. This plan should integrate congregational information, community information, and missional assessment results. It should include action steps toward becoming a more missional congregation, establishing relationships with unchurched people in the community, and giving members the opportunity to connect with the activities of God around the world through informed prayer or short-term mission experiences.

Sail On!

The story of becoming a missional church is still being written. As you set your congregation's course toward becoming missional, you are embarking on an exciting journey: exploring the heart of God for His church in real time. Your traveling companions on this journey are a relatively small number of congregations, modern-day pioneers like yourself.

On this journey, you and your companions must set and constantly monitor your own course. Although in this book I have offered you stories from other journeys, and guideposts along the way, there are no tried-and-true maps. No one can offer a program or plan with seven steps to success in becoming a missional church.

In fact, easy steps toward missional do not exist because every church is unique and every context is different. So the decisions you make must be informed by your church and your community as you seek God's heart.

In this book you have met leaders like yourself. They have attempted to find an appropriate direction to allow their congregation to pursue God's purpose for them. They have not only determined a sense of purpose and mission, but practical action steps that lead toward realization of that purpose. The key to their accomplishment is the practices they have pursued, born of their deep passion for God's missional purpose.

If you wish for a template to follow, consider this: there is a very personal God, whose Spirit lives within you and fellow believers in your church. He desires to accomplish His purpose through you, in your locale. In the quiet places of your heart, He will reveal to you the steps you should pursue in living out His heart's desire. As you hear His voice, have courage and cast off without fear. Even tempests are no challenge to Him.

Sail on!

Reflection and Application

1. Lead your congregation to celebrate its history. Place newsprint around the walls of a large room. Divide the paper into sections according to the eras of your history (in some instances each segment might be a year, in others a decade or other period). Record major events in the appropriate time segments. Invite members to write memories, both high and low points, on the paper in the appropriate time slot. Display the "graph" in a banquet setting, inviting members to share brief accounts of those memories they included on the mural. At the conclusion of the event, unveil a new length of paper and invite members to write their vision of the church's future.

2. Every community is changing. Every church has a life cycle. Ask church leaders to consider actions that could perpetuate effective ministry in the community served by the church into the next century. From their considerations, determine a strategy for ministry beyond the current life expectancy of today's members.

3. The author would love to enter into a dialogue with you. Contact the author by going to Shaped by God's Heart (www.Blogger.com) to sign in, or at minatrea@missional.org.

SUGGESTED READING

Rogers, M. C., and King, C. V. *The Kingdom Agenda: Experiencing God in Your Workplace.* Murfreesboro, Tenn.: Saratoga Press, 1996.
Articles are constantly updated on the Website of the Missional Church Center; please visit us at http://www.bgct.org/missional_church.

APPENDIX: MISSIONAL CHURCH CULTURAL ASSESSMENT

The assessments in each of the missional practice chapters were meant for use with and by individuals. I hope you have been transferring your scores to this section, so you can now get a more comprehensive picture of your church's readiness for moving to missional. This Appendix is intended for use as an evaluation tool by a group consisting of pastor and lay church leaders.

Rating

Rate each statement that follows from 1 (the statement is not true of our church) to 7 (the statement is true of our church) by circling the appropriate response.

Scoring

Write your response in the box to the right of each statement, total your responses, and divide that result by 7. The result is your net response for that practice. Average the responses of all group members to obtain your overall sense of the church's position on each of the nine missional practices.

Evaluating

Observe the items in which group responses reflect significant disagreement. Use disagreement as an opportunity for dialogue concerning the practice. For example, if your group responds uniformly low on a missional practice, this might mean you recognize a need to address an area. A uniformly low response might be quite important, but it may not merit immediate attention because the group perceives the practice as beyond the church's change quotient at this time. You need to feel your way here; there are no absolutes.

Remember: the journey does not take place overnight. Some areas might be addressed months or years later. As a leader, you can work now to begin developing strategy toward those areas, paving the way for more ready adoption down the road.

Missional Practice Number One:
Have a High Threshold for Membership

Circle your response to each statement. Transfer response to box, total, and divide by 7 to find your net response.

We have clearly stated expectations of members.

1   2   3   4   5   6   7   ☐

We clearly communicate pathways to membership.

1   2   3   4   5   6   7   ☐

Members hold one another accountable for fulfilling expectations.

1   2   3   4   5   6   7   ☐

We communicate benefits of membership.

1   2   3   4   5   6   7   ☐

Significant numbers of pre-Christians identify us as their faith community.

1   2   3   4   5   6   7   ☐

We have various entry points through which new members become part of our church.

1   2   3   4   5   6   7   ☐

Nominal Christianity is abnormal in our church.

1   2   3   4   5   6   7   ☐

TOTAL SCORE ☐

Net Response for Missional Practice (divide total score by 7) ☐

Missional Practice Number Two:
Be Real, Not Real Religious

Circle your response to each statement. Transfer response to box, total, and divide by 7 to find your net response.

Our message is validated by our actions in the community.

1   2   3   4   5   6   7 ☐

Members do not "wear masks" with one another.

1   2   3   4   5   6   7 ☐

People in the community see our church as vital.

1   2   3   4   5   6   7 ☐

Members trust one another enough to confess their sin.

1   2   3   4   5   6   7 ☐

Members are incorporated into small groups for growth and accountability.

1   2   3   4   5   6   7 ☐

We prioritize member involvement with unchurched people.

1   2   3   4   5   6   7 ☐

Our culture makes it easy for people to admit unanswered questions about their faith.

1   2   3   4   5   6   7 ☐

TOTAL SCORE ☐

Net Response for Missional Practice (divide total score by 7) ☐

Missional Practice Number Three: Teach to Obey Rather Than to Know

Circle your response to each statement. Transfer response to box, total, and divide by 7 to find your net response.

We have a high regard for the Word of God.

1　　　　2　　　　3　　　　4　　　　5　　　　6　　　　7　　　　☐

Members are equipped to practice spiritual disciplines.

1　　　　2　　　　3　　　　4　　　　5　　　　6　　　　7　　　　☐

Our teaching ministries emphasize moving from knowledge to obedience.

1　　　　2　　　　3　　　　4　　　　5　　　　6　　　　7　　　　☐

We partner new believers with existing members in learning relationships.

1　　　　2　　　　3　　　　4　　　　5　　　　6　　　　7　　　　☐

We challenge members to be responsible in their obedience to God.

1　　　　2　　　　3　　　　4　　　　5　　　　6　　　　7　　　　☐

We excel in equipping members to apply Bible knowledge to real-life situations.

1　　　　2　　　　3　　　　4　　　　5　　　　6　　　　7　　　　☐

We hold one another accountable for obeying God's Word.

1　　　　2　　　　3　　　　4　　　　5　　　　6　　　　7　　　　☐

TOTAL SCORE ☐

Net Response for Missional Practice (divide total score by 7) ☐

Missional Practice Number Four:
Rewrite Worship Every Week

Circle your response to each statement. Transfer response to box, total, and divide by 7 to find your net response.

Our worship focuses on an audience of one.
1   2   3   4   5   6   7   ☐

We use a team of members in planning worship.
1   2   3   4   5   6   7   ☐

Members lead corporate worship through sharing their various talents.
1   2   3   4   5   6   7   ☐

We routinely incorporate new ideas or methods in worship.
1   2   3   4   5   6   7   ☐

We challenge members to be responsible in their obedience to God.
1   2   3   4   5   6   7   ☐

Our worship is designed to use each of the five senses.
1   2   3   4   5   6   7   ☐

Our church prepares members for personal worship experiences.
1   2   3   4   5   6   7   ☐

TOTAL SCORE ☐

Net Response for Missional Practice (divide total score by 7) ☐

Missional Practice Number Five:
Live Apostolically

Circle your response to each statement. Transfer response to box, total, and divide by 7 to find your net response.

Our members consider themselves as missionaries.

| 1 | 2 | 3 | 4 | 5 | 6 | 7 |

Members routinely introduce new believers to faith in Christ.

| 1 | 2 | 3 | 4 | 5 | 6 | 7 |

Members interpret contemporary culture through Biblical guidance.

| 1 | 2 | 3 | 4 | 5 | 6 | 7 |

We encourage members to participate in "secular" social groups.

| 1 | 2 | 3 | 4 | 5 | 6 | 7 |

Our church is transforming the community in which we live.

| 1 | 2 | 3 | 4 | 5 | 6 | 7 |

Members learn to establish and maintain authentic relationships with lost persons.

| 1 | 2 | 3 | 4 | 5 | 6 | 7 |

Members are involved in leading the nations to worship Christ.

| 1 | 2 | 3 | 4 | 5 | 6 | 7 |

TOTAL SCORE

Net Response for Missional Practice (divide total score by 7)

Missional Practice Number Six:
Expect to Change the World

Circle your response to each statement. Transfer response to box, total, and divide by 7 to find your net response.

Members believe our church is making a major difference in the world.

1   2   3   4   5   6   7   ☐

Our church has a vital prayer ministry focusing on updated mission concerns.

1   2   3   4   5   6   7   ☐

Most members have identified their primary mission field.

1   2   3   4   5   6   7   ☐

Our church has strategies for reaching new people groups in our area.

1   2   3   4   5   6   7   ☐

Our members intentionally cultivate global relationships.

1   2   3   4   5   6   7   ☐

Our worship regularly emphasizes the member's missionary involvement.

1   2   3   4   5   6   7   ☐

Most of our members participate in short-term mission projects.

1   2   3   4   5   6   7   ☐

TOTAL SCORE   ☐

Net Response for Missional Practice (divide total score by 7)   ☐

Missional Practice Number Seven:
Order Actions According to Purpose

Circle your response to each statement. Transfer response to box, total, and divide by 7 to find your net response.

Members are very clear about our church's purpose.

1   2   3   4   5   6   7   ☐

We calendar only events that help us to accomplish our purpose.

1   2   3   4   5   6   7   ☐

Our programs are flexible, leaving room for God to direct changes.

1   2   3   4   5   6   7   ☐

We are good at celebrating the starting *and* closing of ministries.

1   2   3   4   5   6   7   ☐

Items in our budget reflect our missional priorities.

1   2   3   4   5   6   7   ☐

Our programs and ministries give evidence of our commitment to excellence.

1   2   3   4   5   6   7   ☐

We would rather lose a prospect than violate our purpose.

1   2   3   4   5   6   7   ☐

TOTAL SCORE ☐

Net Response for Missional Practice (divide total score by 7) ☐

Missional Practice Number Eight:
Measure Growth by Capacity to Release, Not Retain

Circle your response to each statement. Transfer response to box, total, and divide by 7 to find your net response.

We consider it a blessing when we give members to start new churches or ministries.

1   2   3   4   5   6   7

Our church equips disciples to serve as missionaries.

1   2   3   4   5   6   7

Our members believe new churches are needed in our community.

1   2   3   4   5   6   7

We expect members to be "on mission" locally and globally.

1   2   3   4   5   6   7

We regularly commission members who are going into ministry.

1   2   3   4   5   6   7

Our church has an aggressive plan for starting new community ministries and churches.

1   2   3   4   5   6   7

We successfully move new believers into leadership roles.

1   2   3   4   5   6   7

TOTAL SCORE

Net Response for Missional Practice (divide total score by 7)

Missional Practice Number Nine:
Place Kingdom Concerns First

Circle your response to each statement. Transfer response to box, total, and divide by 7 to find your net response.

Our actions evidence our partnership with Christian churches in our community.

1   2   3   4   5   6   7   ☐

We emphasize the communal as well as individual nature of salvation.

1   2   3   4   5   6   7   ☐

We share the pain and joy of Christians around the world.

1   2   3   4   5   6   7   ☐

We intentionally partner with all believers in the work of the Kingdom.

1   2   3   4   5   6   7   ☐

In worship we regularly pray for other churches in our city.

1   2   3   4   5   6   7   ☐

Members participate in spiritual warfare through a vital prayer ministry.

1   2   3   4   5   6   7   ☐

Our members are involved in interdenominational ministries.

1   2   3   4   5   6   7   ☐

TOTAL SCORE   ☐

Net Response for Missional Practice (divide total score by 7)   ☐

NOTES

INTRODUCTION

1. Bosch, David J. *Transforming Mission: Paradigm Shifts in Theology of Mission*. Maryknoll, New York: Orbis Books, 1991, p. 390.

CHAPTER ONE

1. Jamye Miller, interview with author, Irving, Texas, June 7, 2002.

2. Darrell Guder, interview with author, Columbia Theological Seminary, Atlanta, June 26, 2002.

3. Payne, Bishop C. E., and Beazley, H. *Reclaiming the Great Commission: A Practical Model for Transforming Denominations and Congregations*. San Francisco: Jossey-Bass, 2000, p. 23.

4. Riddell, M. *Threshold of the Future: Reforming the Church in the Post-Christian West*. London: Society for Promoting Christian Knowledge, 1998, p. 24.

5. Jimmy Seibert, interview with author, Antioch Community Church, Waco, Texas, May 23, 2002.

6. Charles Van Engen, e-mail correspondence with author, 2000.

7. Nilson Fanini, interview with author, Niterói, Brazil, October 2003.

8. Steinbeck, J. *Travels with Charley in Search of America*. New York: Penguin Books, 1962, p. 4.

9. Van Dyke, H. *Who Owns the Mountains?* Chicago: Northfield, 1995, pp. 24–25.

10. Riddell (1998), p. 13.

CHAPTER TWO

1. Connie Wilson, interview with author, Kansas City, Kansas, May 31, 2002.

2. Dayton, E. R., and Fraser, D. A. *Planning Strategies for World Evangelization*. Grand Rapids, Mich.: Eerdmans, 1990, p. 45.

3. Kirk, J. A. *What Is Mission?: Theological Explorations*. Minneapolis: Fortress Press, 2000, p. 30.

4. Piper, J. *Let the Nations Be Glad!: The Supremacy of God in Missions*. Grand Rapids, Mich.: Baker Books, 1993, p. 11.

5. Stowell, J. M. *Following Christ: Experiencing Life the Way It Was Meant to Be*. Grand Rapids, Mich.: Zondervan, 1996, p. 61.

6. Lewis, R. *The Church of Irresistible Influence*. Grand Rapids, Mich.: Zondervan, 2001, p. 29.

7. Van Engen, C. *God's Missionary People: Rethinking the Purpose of the Local Church*. Grand Rapids, Mich.: Baker Books, 1991, p. 134.

PART TWO

1. Lois Barrett, telephone interview with author, Mar. 2002.

CHAPTER THREE

1. This paradigm is presented as Chapter Seven (by Alan J. Roxburgh) in Guder, D. (ed.). *Missional Church: A Vision for the Sending of the Church in North America*. Grand Rapids, Mich.: Eerdmans, 1998; see especially pp. 201–212.

2. Guder (2000), p. 175.

3. Guder (1998), pp. 244–245.

4. Nominal membership within the Christian church in the West is, in part, the reason for the discrepancy between the number reflected as "affiliated church members" and "church attenders" in David Barrett's *Status of Global Mission, 2000, in Context of 20th and 21st Centuries*. In that annual portrait, the total number of affiliated church members in Christian churches for the year 2000 was 1,888,441,000. However, of those, only 1,359,420,000 were reflected as church attenders. The report continues by listing the number of affiliated church members who are identified as Great Commission Christians, "active church members who take Christ's Great Commission seriously." Alarmingly, that number drops to 647,810,000 (*International Bulletin of Missionary Research*, Jan. 2000). According to Barrett's global research, one must assume only one in three persons identified as Christian take seriously God's missional purpose. This further underscores the implications of nominal membership.

5. Evangelism Processes Colloquium, Wilson World Hotel, Dallas, Texas, August 21, 2001. Sponsored by Church Planting Institute; Fred Ater, convener.

6. *Pilgrim's Progress Guide,* NorthWood Church for the Communities, n.d., p. 27.

7. De Pree, M. *Leading Without Power: Finding Hope in Serving Community.* San Francisco: Jossey-Bass, 1997, p. 57.

8. "Mosaic Life in Church: Leader's Guide," May 25, 2000, pp. 7–8.

9. Erwin McManus, interview with author, Los Angeles, California, Apr. 21, 2002.

CHAPTER FOUR

1. Drane, J. *The McDonaldization of the Church: Consumer Culture and the Church's Future.* Macon, Ga.: Smyth and Helwys, 2001, p. 82.

2. Kotlowitz, A. *There Are No Children Here: The Story of Two Boys Growing up in the Other America.* New York: Doubleday, 1991, p. 143; emphasis added.

3. Lewis (2001), p. 40.

4. Stowell (1996), p. 86.

5. Yaconelli, M. *Dangerous Wonder: The Adventure of Childlike Faith.* Colorado Springs: NavPress, 1998, p. 53.

6. Cole, N. *Cultivating a Life for God.* Carol Stream, Ill.: ChurchSmart Resources, 1999, p. 63.

7. From "Toolkit," in *Antioch Leadership Notebook,* n.d.

8. Lewis (2001), p. 41.

9. Tichy, Noel M., with Cohen, E. *The Leadership Engine: How Winning Companies Build Leaders at Every Level.* New York: HarperBusiness, 1997, p. 111.

10. *Pilgrim's Progress Guide,* p. 47.

11. Herrington, J., Bonem, M., and Furr, J. H. *Leading Congregational Change: A Practical Guide for the Transformational Journey.* San Francisco: Jossey-Bass, 2000, p. 27.

CHAPTER FIVE

1. Wallis, J. *Faith Works: Lessons from the Life of an Activist Preacher.* New York: Random House, 2000, pp. xxvii–xxviii.

2. Jeff Harris, interview with author, San Antonio, Texas, Apr. 4, 2002.

3. Bob Roberts, interview with author, Keller, Texas, Apr. 11, 2002.

4. McManus (2002).

5. McManus, E. R. *An Unstoppable Force: Daring to Become the Church God Had in Mind*. Loveland, Colo.: Group Publishing, 2001, pp. 71–72.

6. Rhodes, L. N., and Richardson, N. D. *Mending Severed Connections: Theological Education for Communal Transformation*. San Francisco: San Francisco Network Ministries, 1991, p. 64.

7. This is the framework upon which Richard Foster fashions his treatment of spiritual disciplines. See Foster, R. *Celebration of Discipline: The Path to Spiritual Growth*. San Francisco: Harper and Row, 1978.

8. Guder (2002).

9. Beckham, W. A. *The Second Reformation: Reshaping the Church for the 21st Century*. Houston: Touch, 1997, p. 126.

10. Moore, W. B. *Multiplying Disciples*. Colorado Springs: NavPress, 1981, p. 112.

11. All excerpts are from Grace Point Church's self-published *Discovery Guidebook*, n.d.

12. Van Engen (1991), p. 153.

13. Quoted in Peterson, E. H. *A Long Obedience in the Same Direction*. Downers Grove, Ill.: Intervarsity Press, 1980, p. 13.

14. Hanks, B., and Shell, W. A. (eds.) *Discipleship: Great Insights from the Most Experienced Disciple Makers*. Grand Rapids, Mich.: Zondervan, 1981.

Chapter Six

1. Pine, B. J., II, and Gilmore, J. H. "Welcome to the Experience Economy." *Harvard Business Review,* July–Aug 1998, p. 102.

2. Piper (1993), p. 45.

3. Palin, M. *Full Circle: One Man's Journey by Air, Train, Boat, and Occasionally Very Sore Feet Around the 50,000 Miles of the Pacific Rim*. New York: St. Martin's Press, 1997, p. 60.

4. Lewis, C. S. *Letters to Malcolm: Chiefly on Prayer*. Orlando: Harcourt Brace, 1964, p. 4.

5. McManus (2002).

6. "The Dick Staub Interview: Chris Seay." *Christianity Today,* Sept. 24, 2002. (http://www.christianitytoday.com/ct/2002/137/21.0html)

7. McManus (2002).

8. Riddell (1998), p. 31.

9. Drane (2001), p. 17.

CHAPTER SEVEN

1. "Chris Seay" (2002).

2. Van Gelder, C. *The Essence of the Church: A Community Created by the Spirit.* Grand Rapids, Mich.: Baker Books, 2000, pp. 168–169.

3. Fish, R. J., and Conant, J. E. *Every Member Evangelism for Today.* New York: HarperCollins, 1976, p. 9.

4. Riddell (1998), pp. 24 and 27.

5. R. Lewis (2001), p. 39.

6. "Chris Seay" (2002).

7. McLaren, B. D. *The Church on the Other Side: Doing Ministry in the Postmodern Matrix.* Grand Rapids, Mich.: Zondervan, 2000, pp. 181–182.

8. Hunter III, G. G. *Church for the Unchurched.* Nashville, Tenn.: Abingdon Press, 1996, p. 28.

9. Engel, J. F., and Dryness, W. A. *Changing the Mind of Missions: Where Have We Gone Wrong?* Downers Grove, Ill.: Intervarsity Press, 2000, p. 100.

10. Matt Hannan, interview with author, Vancouver, Washington, Apr. 30, 2002.

CHAPTER EIGHT

1. Komisar, R. *The Monk and the Riddle: The Art of Creating a Life While Making a Living.* Boston: Harvard Business School Press, 2001, p. 76.

2. Bishop Taylor is quoted in Stott, J. *Involvement: Being a Responsible Christian in a Non-Christian Society.* Old Tappan, N.J.: Revell, 1985, p. 93.

3. Hannan (2002).

4. For information on *FirstView,* visit www.percept.info.com.

CHAPTER NINE

1. Warren, R. *The Purpose Driven Life: What on Earth Am I Here For?* Grand Rapids, Mich.: Zondervan, 2002, pp. 312–313.

2. Drucker, P. F. *Managing the Nonprofit Organization.* New York: HarperCollins, 1990, p. 4.

3. McManus (2002).

4. Drucker, P. F. *Management Challenges for the 21st Century.* New York: HarperCollins, 1999, p. 74.

5. Seibert (2002).

6. Drucker (1999), p. 74.

7. McManus (2002).

8. Seibert (2002).

CHAPTER TEN

1. Tinsley, W. C. *Upon This Rock: Dimensions of Church Planting.* Atlanta: Home Mission Board, 1985, p. 23.

2. Tinsley (1985), p. 17.

3. Schwarz, C. *Natural Church Development: A Guide to Eight Essential Qualities of Healthy Churches.* Carol Stream, Ill.: ChurchSmart Resources, 1998, p. 10.

4. McLaren (2000), p. 140.

5. Camp, K. "Church Called to Rediscover Its 'Essential Character' in Missions." *Baptist Standard, 113*(14), Apr. 2, 2001, p. 7.

6. Schwarz, C., and Schalk, C. *Implementation Guide to Natural Church Development.* Carol Stream, Ill.: ChurchSmart Resources, p. 137.

7. Allen, R. *The Spontaneous Expansion of the Church.* Grand Rapids, Mich.: Eerdmans, 1962 (reprinted 1978), p. 96.

8. Carol Davis, interview with author, U.S. Center for World Missions, Pasadena, California, April 22, 2002.

9. Seibert (2002).

10. Guder (1998), p. 218.

11. Seibert (2002).

12. Seibert (2002).

13. Wolfgang Simson, personal e-mail, Aug. 31, 2001.

14. Chaney, C. *Church Planting at the End of the Twentieth Century.* Carol Stream, Ill.: Tyndale, 1993, pp. 18–19.

15. Tinsley (1985), p. 25.

CHAPTER ELEVEN

1. Hannan (2002).

2. Lewis, C. S. *Mere Christianity.* San Francisco: HarperSanFrancisco, 1980, p. 46.

3. Fenelon, F. *Christian Perfection*. Minneapolis: Bethany Fellowship, 1975, p. 27.

4. Miller (2002).

5. Miller (2002).

6. Wolfgang Simson, dialogue with postmodern learning community, Austin, Tex., Aug. 27, 2001.

7. Roberts (2002).

8. Hunsberger, George R. "Missional Vocation: Called and Sent to Represent the Reign of God." In Guder, D. (ed.) *Missional Church: A Vision for the Sending of the Church in North America*. Grand Rapids, Mich.: Eerdmans, 1998, p. 95.

9. Hunsberger (1998), p. 95.

10. Linthicum, R. *City of God, City of Satan: A Biblical Theology of the Urban Church*. Grand Rapids, Mich.: Zondervan, 1991, pp. 98–99.

11. Dayton and Fraser (1990), p. 45.

12. Linthicum (1991), p. 105.

13. Riddell (1998), p. 37.

14. Harris (2002).

15. Bosch (1991), p. 465.

16. Ward, T. "Repositioning Mission Agencies for the Twenty-First Century." *International Bulletin of Missionary Research*, 1999, 23(4), p. 149.

17. Garrett, L. "Heritage." (http://www.freedomsring.org/heritage/chap6.html)

18. Hook, C. "Introduction to Heritage." (http://www.freedomsring.org/heritage/intro.html)

19. "Fridge flyer." New Heights Church, Vancouver, Wash., Apr. 28, 2002.

20. Jim Herrington is quoted in Dennison, J. *City Reaching: On the Road to Community Transformation*. Pasadena, Calif.: William Carey Library, 1999, pp. 106–107.

21. Van Gelder (2000), pp. 99–100.

CHAPTER THIRTEEN

1. Drucker is quoted in Jennings, J., and Haughton, L. *It's Not the Big That Eat the Small . . . It's the Fast That Eat the Slow: How to Use Speed as a Competitive Tool in Business*. New York: HarperBusiness, 2000, p. 15.

2. McManus (2001), p. 74.

3. McNeal, R. *A Work of Heart*. San Francisco: Jossey-Bass, 2000, p. 19.

4. Used by permission from *Community and Church Leaders Join Forces in Northeast Houston,* a Web-based article published by Mission Houston, Jim Herrington, executive director, May 6, 2003.

5. Lawrence, Brother, and Laubach, F. *Practicing His Presence.* Sargent, Ga.: SeedSowers, 1973, p. 85.

6. Tozer, A. W. *The Best of A. W. Tozer.* Grand Rapids, Mich.: Baker Book House, 1978, p. 61.

7. McNeal (2000), p. 13.

8. Quinn, R. E. *Deep Change: Discovering the Leader Within.* San Francisco: Jossey-Bass, 1996, p. 3.

9. McManus (2002).

10. McManus (2001), p. 128.

11. Harris (2002).

12. Sweet, L. *AquaChurch.* Loveland, Colo.: Group Publishing, 1999, p. 95.

13. McManus (2002).

14. Hannan (2002).

15. Gladwell, M. *The Tipping Point: How Little Things Can Make a Big Difference.* Boston: Little, Brown, 2000, pp. 255–256.

16. Seibert (2002).

17. De Pree, M. *Leadership Is an Art.* New York: Dell, 1989, pp. 11–12.

18. Herrington, Bonem, and Furr (2000) offer excellent insights into this issue (p. 101).

CHAPTER FOURTEEN

1. Among the most popular are Kouzes and Posner's Leadership Practices Inventory (LPI) and LEAD (Leader Effectiveness and Adaptability Description). Both instruments are available from University Associates, Inc., 8517 Production Ave., San Diego, CA 92121. Less comprehensive are the "iLead" and "iChange" inventories, available online (www.Perceptnet.com).

About Leadership Network

The mission of Leadership Network is to accelerate the effectiveness of the Church by identifying and connecting strategic leaders and providing them with access to resources in the form of new ideas, people, and tools.

Leadership Network's focus has been on the practice and application of faith at the local congregational level. Churches and church leaders served by Leadership Network represent a wide variety of primarily Protestant faith traditions that range from mainline to evangelical to independent. All are characterized by innovation, entrepreneurial leadership, and a desire to be on the leading edge of ministry.

Established as a private foundation in 1984 by social entrepreneur Bob Buford, Leadership Network is acknowledged as an influential leader among churches and faith-based ministries and a major resource to which innovative leaders turn for networking and information.

For additional information on Leadership Network, please contact

Leadership Network
2501 Cedar Springs, Suite 200
Dallas, Texas 75201
800.765.5323
www.leadnet.org

THE AUTHOR

MILFRED MINATREA is a contemplative whose passion is intimacy with God. A missiologist and urban strategist, Minatrea is director of the Missional Church Center for Baptist General Convention of Texas. He previously served as director of the Church and Community Ministries Division for Dallas Baptist Association and pastored churches in Texas. He earned a doctor of ministry in missions administration degree from Golden Gate Baptist Theological Seminary and has taught undergraduate courses in Urban Ministry.

He enjoys assisting churches in equipping members for their roles in God's missional purpose. A practitioner in ministry, Minatrea consults with churches in strategic visioning and frequently serves churches as interim pastor. Minatrea enjoys walking the streets of the world's urban centers, finding wonderful "hole-in-the-wall (mom and pop) restaurants"; playing golf (rather poorly); pampering his '64 Volkswagen Karman Ghia; and reading travel essays, good mysteries, and the biographies of people he would like to have known. Beyond loving his family, he is passionate about *being real* as an authentic disciple of Jesus and walking with others on that journey.